MW00437755

Birding Hot Spots
of Central New Mexico

Number Forty-two
W. L. Moody Jr. Natural History Series

A⫪M nature guides

Greater Roadrunner
Photo by Laurel Ladwig

TEXAS A&M UNIVERSITY PRESS   COLLEGE STATION

Birding Hot Spots of Central New Mexico

Judy Liddell & Barbara Hussey

Photographs by Judy Liddell unless otherwise indicated

This paper meets the requirements
of ANSI/NISO Z39.48-1992
(Permanence of Paper).
Binding materials have been chosen for durability.

LIBRARY OF CONGRESS CATALOGING-IN-PUBLICATION DATA

Liddell, Judy, 1942–
Birding hot spots of central New Mexico / Judy Liddell and Barbara Hussey ;
photographs by Judy Liddell unless otherwise indicated.—1st ed.
    p. cm.—(W. L. Moody Jr. natural history series ; no. 42)
    Includes bibliographical references and index.
    ISBN-13: 978-1-60344-426-2 (pb-flexibound : alk. paper)
    ISBN-10: 1-60344-426-2 (pb-flexibound : alk. paper)
    ISBN-13: 978-1-60344-668-6 (e-book)
    ISBN-10: 1-60344-668-0 (e-book)
    1. Bird watching—New Mexico—Guidebooks.
2. Birds—New Mexico—Guidebooks.
I. Hussey, Barbara, 1946- II. Title. III. Series: W.L. Moody, Jr.,
natural history series ; no. 42.
    QL684.N6L44   2011
    598.072'34789—dc22
    2011005236

*The book is dedicated
to all of the bird species
of central New Mexico
that have provided us
with so much
joy & inspiration.*

Table of Contents

List of Maps

Preface

This guide is a true collaboration between Judy Liddell and Barbara Hussey. Whereas the New Mexico Ornithological Society's excellent *New Mexico Bird Finding Guide* covers the entire state, this guide seeks to provide a more in-depth look at birding hot spots in the state's central region. It should be considered a supplemental handbook.

> *To watch a bird is to know the world in a completely different way.*
>
> Steve Braunias,
> New Zealand author, *To Watch a Bird*

I would not be an avid birder if it had not been for my friend Barbara, who hung a seed bell and suet feeder next to my window a number of years ago when I was recuperating from knee-replacement surgery. When a Curve-billed Thrasher came to the suet block, I was amazed by my close-up look at its bill and throat and was hooked. As I eased back into outdoor activities, birding was the perfect entree. I would drive to the Rio Grande Nature Center State Park, sit on a bench, and study the birds. When I retired and started birding weekly with Central New Mexico Audubon's Thursday Birders, I became aware of many more locations where I could enjoy birds. Early in 2007 I launched "It's a Bird Thing" (www.wingandsong.wordpress.com) to share my passion for birds. Through the blog, I began to get inquiries from out-of-state birders about where to find specific species when they visited New Mexico.

The seeds for this guide were sown by fellow birders Dave and Abby Watson from Hawaii, who were spending part of the year in Albuquerque. "You're a writer. You should write a guidebook," they encouraged me. I spent the next year taking notes each week and posting information about sites and birds on my blog.

I knew that this book would not be all it could be without involvement from Barbara and asked her to be a coauthor. I was delighted when she accepted enthusiastically. As we traveled together to another state, we began making notes on what was helpful and missing from other bird-finding guides. One of our discoveries was that since most existing guides are written by men, no thought was given to where to find a restroom at remote locations. We researched this information for each site. Another addition, based on our work experience in the disabilities field, is the accessibility of each site. Since we both often have gone birding in connection with business travel when we might not have a car, we included instructions for traveling to sites by public transportation, when available.

As I began to write, I returned to each site many times to check details. It was a labor of love; however, as I use other guides in my travels, I truly appreciate the work that goes into assuring that a bird-finding guide is accurate and thorough.

The experience of writing this book has been enriching and has given me a renewed appreciation of the wide variety of birds and habitats in central New Mexico.

—Judy Liddell
Albuquerque, New Mexico

Years ago, on a Fourth of July, I stood watching my then toddler son, Tom, ride a miniature train with his grandmother in a Florida state park. My brother, Paul, a recent birding "convert," handed me his binoculars and pointed to what seemed to me an unremarkable, brownish bird in a nearby tree. As I struggled to focus the unfamiliar glasses, I was surprised to notice the dull brown bird had an interesting black mustache, polka dots on its chest, and maybe even red feathers behind its head. The bird suddenly took to the air, briefly revealing its brilliant yellow wings—my first Northern (Yellow-shafted) Flicker and the first bird of my newfound fascination called a "life list." I had discovered the thrill of birding. Decades later it still, of course, thrills me to see a new bird or even find an old familiar one.

Through the years, birding has also allowed me to gain awareness for other aspects of the natural world. After starting this agreeable journey in Florida, I followed my husband, Tom, and our growing family to the enthralling beauty of New Mexico and now, very recently, bustling northern Virginia, but not before visiting many wonderful places in the world and their amazing birds and landscapes. Over time my family learned to tolerate my obsession for wild things and maybe picked up a healthy appreciation for nature along the way.

When my friend Judy asked me to work with her writing *Birding Hot Spots of Central New Mexico*, I jumped at the chance. Here was a concrete opportunity to help others discover the bird life of the home I loved for so many years. Sharing Judy's enthusiastic approach to our favorite pastime has been, and continues to be, an extraordinary pleasure.

—Barbara Hussey
Arlington, Virginia

Acknowledgments

We are deeply grateful to Shannon Davies, Louise Lindsey Merrick Editor for the Natural Environment, Texas A&M University Press, for seeing the potential in this book and for her continual support and encouragement through each stage of the publishing process.

This guide has been enriched through the generous contributions of numerous central New Mexico birders who shared their wealth of information about local sites and species. Thanks to the following individuals who shared their knowledge: Mary Lou Arthur, Bosque Bill, Karen and Gary Boettcher, Elsa Bumstead, Steve and Nancy Cox, Sylvia Fee, Rebecca Gracey, Roger Grimshaw, Linda Heinze, Michael Hilchey, Lee Hopwood, Melissa Howard, Bonnie Long, Lannois Neely, Cheri Orwig, Gale Owings, Christopher Rustay, Sei Tokuda, Raymond Van Buskirk, Sondra Williamson, and Charlie Wood. We apologize if we have unintentionally omitted anyone.

Thanks also go to Bonnie Long for her generous use of a number of photographs depicting a variety of bird species and to Laurel Ladwig for the cover and title page photographs, plus Williamson's sapsucker banding.

The content of a number of site descriptions was informed from the thorough information maintained by Ken Schneider on his rosyfinch.com Web page. Beverly McFarland, a specialist on plants in the Sandia Mountains, provided information about poison ivy in New Mexico. John Fleck, *Albuquerque Journal* science writer, helped explain the terminology used to describe silvery minnow and cottonwood habitat restoration. Linda Hussey assisted with research on safety, trail maps, street directions, food, and lodging. Bill Burk III, architect, helped with evaluating accessibility.

Thanks are due to all of the diligent birders who have entered their central New Mexico sightings, including numbers, into eBird. These sightings formed the basis of the birds mentioned at individual site descriptions, as well as the annotated checklist.

We are grateful for the input from a number of local, state, and federal agencies and nonprofit organizations.

The following individuals from Albuquerque's Open Space Division lent their expertise to the site descriptions located in the Open Space areas: Jodi

Hedderig, Open Space Visitor Center manager; James Lewis, associate planner; William Pentler, Open Space parks specialist–education coordinator; James Satler, visitor services and resource management supervisor; Kent Swanson, associate planner; Joshua Willis, Open Space coordinator; and Eric Zsemlye, bosque forestry specialist.

Michael Jaramillo, street and Open Space director for the Village of Los Lunas Parks and Recreation, provided a review of the River Park site description.

Ted Hodoba, project manager, Whitfield Conservation Area, supplied essential details of the new site to assure its inclusion in this guide.

Colleen Langan, Open Space coordinator, and Clay Campbell, planning manager for Bernalillo County Open Space, reviewed the material about Ojito de San Antonio Open Space.

Dan J. Williams, editor, *New Mexico Wildlife*, oversaw the input from New Mexico Department of Game and Fish for Bernardo Wildlife Management Area. Karen Herzenburg, instructional coordinator, reviewed and provided recommendations on Rio Grande Nature Center State Park.

A number of individuals from Cibola National Forest added to the various sections that fall within both the Sandia and Mountainair Ranger Districts: Cid H. Morgan, district ranger, Sandia Ranger District; Susan A. Johnson, Recreation Special Uses–Developed Sites–Fees–Volunteer Management, Sandia District; Lisa L. Jones, Trails & Wilderness Program manager, Sandia District; and Arlene T. Perea, recreation technician, Mountainair District Ranger Station. Hart R. Schwarz, neotropical bird specialist, Cibola National Forest, shared data from breeding-bird surveys and his extensive knowledge of bird species at Salinas and Petroglyph National Monuments.

Diane Souter, chief of interpretation and outreach, Petroglyph National Monument, reviewed the two site descriptions within the monument.

Shawn G. Gillette, supervisory outdoor recreation planner, Bosque del Apache National Wildlife Refuge; and Leigh Ann Vradenburg, executive director, Friends of Bosque del Apache, contributed to the description of the refuge.

We are grateful to Steve Braunias for granting us permission to use the quotation from his book, *How to Watch a Bird*, which so aptly describes how birds have provided us a wonderful lens through which to see the world around us.

Thanks go to our copyeditor, Cynthia Lindlof, for her sharp eye and discerning questions that added to the guide's clarity.

We owe our deep gratitude to Christiana Burk, who generously lent her architectural skills and many hours of labor to create the trail and driving maps, including numerous iterations and changes. Many thanks to Pat Clabaugh, project editor, for guiding and advising through the production process.

Birding Hot Spots
of Central New Mexico

◀◀ ▶▶

CHAPTER 1

Central New Mexico's Geography, Life Zones, and Habitats

Central New Mexico is a premier destination for birders. Over 240 species can be found regularly from the Rio Grande bosque to the tops of the Sandia Mountains and include such specialties as all three species of rosy-finch and thousands of Sandhill Cranes that winter in the area. The region's habitat diversity provides an opportunity to observe such unique species as Crissal Thrasher, Bewick's Wren, and American Three-toed Woodpecker all in the same day.

This chapter describes the area of New Mexico where the sites in this book are located as well as habitat terminology used in the site descriptions.

Geography

The sites covered in this guide are in the greater Albuquerque area—along the Rio Grande from Corrales just north of Albuquerque to the Bosque del Apache National Wildlife Refuge (NWR) just south of Socorro, as well as sites in the Sandia, Manzanita, and Manzano Mountains and foothills. These sites can easily be visited from a base in Albuquerque. Because of their popularity with central New Mexico birders, most have been designated "eBird Hotspots." See "Local Birding Information and Resources" in chapter 2 for a more detailed explanation.

The described sites are divided into six geographic areas: along the Rio Grande in Albuquerque and Corrales; Sandia Foothills; Sandia Mountains; Manzanita and Manzano Mountains; Petroglyph National Monument; and south of Albuquerque. The sites are located in five counties: Bernalillo,

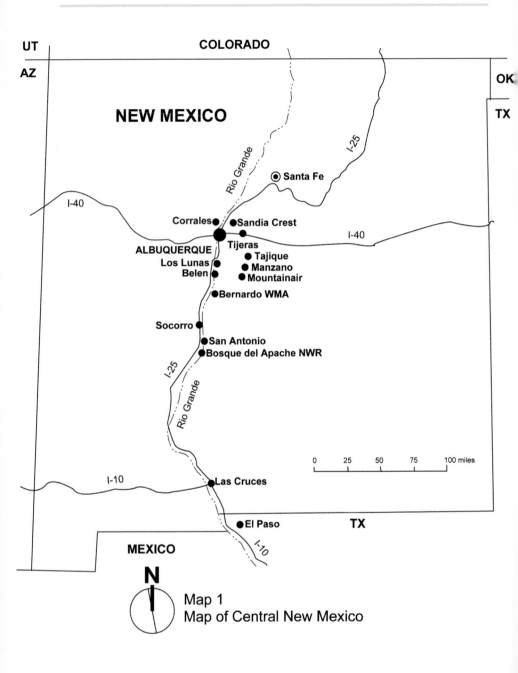

Map 1
Map of Central New Mexico

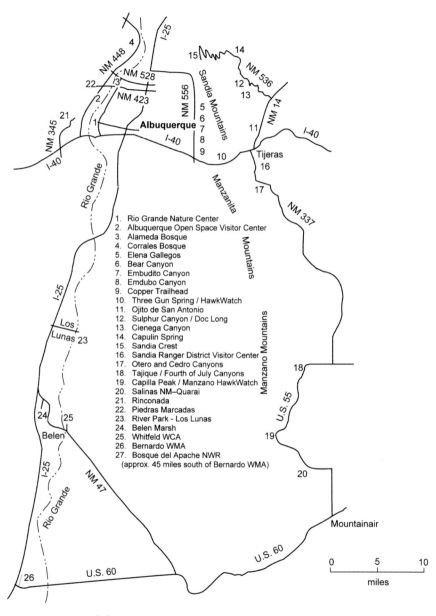

1. Rio Grande Nature Center
2. Albuquerque Open Space Visitor Center
3. Alameda Bosque
4. Corrales Bosque
5. Elena Gallegos
6. Bear Canyon
7. Embudito Canyon
8. Emdubo Canyon
9. Copper Trailhead
10. Three Gun Spring / HawkWatch
11. Ojito de San Antonio
12. Sulphur Canyon / Doc Long
13. Cienega Canyon
14. Capulin Spring
15. Sandia Crest
16. Sandia Ranger District Visitor Center
17. Otero and Cedro Canyons
18. Tajique / Fourth of July Canyons
19. Capilla Peak / Manzano HawkWatch
20. Salinas NM–Quarai
21. Rinconada
22. Piedras Marcadas
23. River Park - Los Lunas
24. Belen Marsh
25. Whitfeld WCA
26. Bernardo WMA
27. Bosque del Apache NWR
    (approx. 45 miles south of Bernardo WMA)

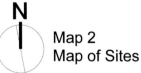

Map 2
Map of Sites

Sandoval, Torrance, Valencia, and Socorro. The map shows where each of the sites is located.

Life Zones and Habitats

Central New Mexico is blessed with a variety of habitats that occur across six of the seven "life zones" and contribute to the rich biodiversity. The concept of life zones, developed by biologist C. Hart Merriam in 1889, is used primarily in the western United States to describe the different plant and animal communities that exist at latitudinal zones with differing temperature and moisture conditions. Every 1,000-foot gain in altitude results in a 3-degree drop in temperature and usually an increase in annual precipitation. For instance, Albuquerque receives an average of 8 inches of precipitation per year, whereas 33 inches may fall on Sandia Crest.

New Mexico's life zones include desert or lower Sonoran—represented in New Mexico by the Chihuahuan Desert (3,000–4,500 feet above sea level)— grassland or upper Sonoran (4,500–5,500 feet), piñon-juniper woodlands (5,000–7,000 feet), transitional or ponderosa pine (6,500–8,500 feet), mixed conifer (8,000–9,500 feet), and spruce-fir (9,000–11,000 feet). Some of these zones have areas of overlap, or ecotones, where species intermingle, often supporting a wider variety of bird species.

The concept of habitat, or plant communities, is much broader and takes into account slope exposure, prevailing winds, and availability of moisture in addition to altitude and latitude. New Mexico Avian Conservation Partners, a collaboration of more than 14 governmental and nonprofit organizations, plus university and private researchers, recognizes the following types of habitats found in central New Mexico. The list has been modified slightly in this guide for ease in locating specific bird species.

- Spruce-fir forest: Dominant plant species are Engelmann spruce, blue spruce, bristlecone pine, and corkbark fir. Sandia Crest and the HawkWatch site at Capilla Peak are located in this habitat.
- Mixed conifer forest: Primary plant species are Douglas-fir, white fir, ponderosa pine, aspen, water birch, Rocky Mountain juniper, and southwestern white pine. Capulin Spring and the meadow below Capilla Peak are examples of this habitat.

- Transition or ponderosa pine forest: The trees include ponderosa pine in an open forest with grassy openings, Gambel oak, western chokecherry, and New Mexican locust. Sites in this type of habitat include Sulphur Canyon and Doc Long Picnic Areas, Cienega Canyon, and Fourth of July Canyon.
- Piñon-juniper woodland: Dominant plant species are piñon pine, juniper, Apache plume, mountain mahogany, and four-wing saltbush. This habitat can be found at Ojito de San Antonio Open Space.
- Montane riparian: Occurs as a narrow, often dense grove of broad-leaved, deciduous trees. Fourth of July Canyon, where bigtooth maples grow, is an example of this type of riparian area.
- Montane shrub: Habitat is a patch or a strip within other more extensive types of vegetation, such as wash, arroyo, or escarpment, where there is less available moisture than in surrounding areas. There are sections of montane shrub along Tajique Canyon.
- Middle-elevation riparian: A tree- and/or shrub-dominated area along a river or stream, including the cottonwood bosque. Examples include all of the sites along the middle Rio Grande, Ojito de San Antonio Open Space, Cedro Nature Trail, and Salinas Pueblo Missions National Monument–Quarai Unit.
- Subalpine meadow: Seasonally wet area at high elevations below the tree line. Examples include the meadow near Kiwanis Cabin at Sandia Crest and the wet, grassy areas near the 10K Trailheads (both north and south).
- Wetlands and lakes: Seasonal and permanent wetlands, marshes, ponds, and lakes. This habitat exists in a number of sites, including parts of Alameda Open Space, Rio Grande Nature Center State Park, Manzano Pond, Belen Marsh, Whitfield Wildlife Conservation Area, Bernardo Wildlife Management Area, and Bosque del Apache NWR.
- Chihuahuan or upland desert scrub (referred to in this guide as desert scrub): Dominated by sand sagebrush in combination with other shrubs and cacti, such as four-wing saltbush, chamisa (rabbit brush), and prickly pear and cholla cacti. This is the primary habitat in all of the sites in the Sandia Foothills and the Petroglyph National Monument.

- Agricultural: Includes areas where crops are planted and harvested. Sites with agricultural areas include Whitfield Wildlife Conservation Area, Bernardo Wildlife Management Area, and Bosque del Apache NWR.

Site descriptions utilize the concept of life zones in the areas of the Sandia and Manzanita/Manzano Mountains. Most of the other site descriptions refer to the type of habitat.

▶ CHAPTER 2

Helpful Information

How to Use This Guide

The directions in this guide are intended to be used in conjunction with a map of New Mexico. Readers will also benefit from a map of Albuquerque for the sites around the city. State maps are available at New Mexico Tourism Department offices. Several, including interactive maps in the form of PDF files, can be downloaded at newmexico.org/map/index.php. This is particularly important when planning to visit one of the sites described in chapter 3, since there are few roads that provide access from one side of the river to the other. All of the written descriptions start from the intersection of Interstate 40 (I-40) and Interstate 25 (I-25).

Six chapters are devoted to distinct areas within central New Mexico: chapter 3 covers four sites on both sides of the Rio Grande north of I-40; chapter 4 describes five sites along the west slope of the Sandia Mountains and one that is accessed from Tijeras Pass; chapter 5 highlights five specific sites at different elevations and describes possible stops while traveling up the mountain; chapter 6 describes six sites along the east slope of the Manzanita and Manzano Mountains; chapter 7 highlights two sites in the geologically distinct Petroglyph National Monument; and chapter 8 describes five sites in the two counties south of Albuquerque, ending with the well-known Bosque del Apache National Wildlife Refuge.

Each description includes general highlights of the site and recommended route; target species; listing of other birds that might be seen by season; driving directions and public transportation route if available; parking; fees; special considerations and hazards; facility information, including accessibility and availability of restrooms, water, and picnic facilities; and general information on the nearest food and lodging.

The seasons for each of the sites are broken down into winter (generally December–March), summer (generally June–August), and migration, which can overlap these two seasons. Spring migration can begin for some species near the end of February and last through May. Fall migration can begin as early as mid-July and end in late November, depending on the species. As you read the list of species at a specific site and find one that is a target species for you, it is wise to check the annotated checklist near the back of the book, where specific months are provided for arrival and departure.

At many sites, we suggest specific clues for locating a species, for example, a plant or geologic/human-made structure. This is not meant to suggest that the species can only be found on that plant or structure.

For definitions of words commonly used in the field of birding, please refer to a field guide of birds of North America. Subspecies of some birds are important to birders. Where more than one subspecies is possible at a site, the specific subspecies will be indicated. The annotated checklist in this book provides subspecies information. If no subspecies is mentioned, for example, for Western Scrub-Jay, it can be assumed that the "Woodhouse's" form is the one found in this region.

Weather and Altitude

It seems no matter what preconceived ideas a person has about New Mexico, the first-time visitor frequently is surprised. When someone is traveling at 65 or 70 miles per hour on an interstate highway, central New Mexico seems monochromatically brown, arid, and dusty. Upon a closer look, the subtleties of its cottonwood-edged valleys and evergreen-shaded or snow-covered mountain trails become apparent. For those who envision Albuquerque as a parched desert, the cool, verdant haven of nearby Sandia Crest can be startling.

Central New Mexico is blessed with an abundance of sun, but snowy winter days are not uncommon. At an altitude of 5,000 to 6,000 feet above sea level, Albuquerque has annual high and low temperatures ranging from an average of 92°F to 65°F in July and 48°F to 24°F in January. At 10,678 feet, Sandia Crest has average temperatures that are a little different, varying from 66°F to 47°F in July and 28°F to 12°F in January. As in most high deserts, the difference in temperature between day and night is significant. New

Mexico's thinner atmosphere and low humidity allow the sun-heated air to escape into space on most nights, but not without the breathtaking reward of a sky full of stars. Albuquerque's average annual rainfall is less than 9 inches, while the adjacent mountains receive over 25 inches of precipitation.

We recommend that you prepare for central New Mexico's variable weather by dressing in layers. It is important to wear a hat with a brim because of the intense sun and to apply sunscreen conscientiously. Long pants and sturdy shoes help ward off cactus thorns and other prickly desert plants, as well as provide traction on loose granite trails. If you plan to visit Sandia Crest in winter seeking rosy-finches, be aware that you may find yourself walking on icy pavement. Mountain trails can be snowy as early as October and as late as May. The snow may linger in the mountains between storms, but valley and foothill areas can experience a storm one day and all evidence will be gone the next.

Check the media (newspapers, broadcast, Internet) for impending weather changes both winter and summer. The late-summer weather pattern of regular afternoon thunderstorms is known as the monsoon season, often accompanied by lightning and flash floods. When storms are nearby, avoid hiking, driving, or parking in arroyos, even if dry. It may be sunny at your location, but an upstream deluge could fill a dry wash in seconds. Conversely, you may see rain falling as virga, vanishing completely before it touches the ground. High winds in the spring increase the danger in montane forested areas from falling trees killed by insect infestation. Stay clear of leaning timber or broken limbs. Rio Grande cottonwoods are considered a self-pruning tree species, so watch for falling branches in the valley as well.

After you fly in from sea level, catching your breath while hiking at 10,000 feet may not be as easy as expected. Sometimes the difference is noticed even at 5,000 feet. Altitude sickness is best avoided by staying hydrated. In the extremely dry air, you are unaware of the perspiration evaporating directly from your skin. Carry water in the mountains, valleys, and deserts—and drink it! Consider all surface water sources to be contaminated.

Safety, Animals, and Pests

A few of the sites in this guide are a considerable distance from gas stations. Start with a full tank, especially in the areas along the Manzanita and Manzano Mountains. Other driving cautions include icy roads; unexpected mountain road closures in winter (or possible tire-chain requirement); and deep, impassable, muddy ruts in dirt roads after summer rains. High-clearance or four-wheel-drive vehicles may be required at some sites in this guide.

While central New Mexico's low humidity levels keep the biting-insect and mite populations low, mosquitoes are found along the river, especially in late summer. Any gnats encountered are easily warded off with long sleeves and, possibly, insect repellent. Chiggers are known to occur at Los Lunas River Park. Tucking your pant legs inside your socks will minimize their siege. Bees, yellow jackets, and wasps can be found along any of the trails described in this guide. You literally may stumble upon an occasional harvester anthill in the Sandia Foothills and along the Rio Grande valley. Their firelike sting can leave welts that last for days. Before standing still to view a bird, look down to make sure you are not standing on an anthill.

Poison ivy grows in New Mexico. The western species *Toxicodendron rydbergii* is the nonclimbing variety. It is known to be present at the Ojito

Western species of poison ivy

de San Antonio Open Space, along the path in Sulphur Canyon Picnic Area in the Sandia Mountains, and in sections of the Cedro Creek Nature Trail in Otero Canyon, among other places in the state.

Several species of rattlesnakes occur in central New Mexico. It is probable that you will never see one. On the other hand, when alarmed, they can generate a buzzing rattle that might be mistaken for a wren or chat vocalization. Avoid advancing unless you are certain you are not walking toward a rattlesnake poised to strike.

Black bears are a concern at some of the birding sites listed. It is important not to leave food unattended on picnic tables, even briefly. The U.S. Forest Service has been known to confiscate abandoned food. Never behave like prey and run from a black bear. Back up slowly and walk away. Similarly, running from a cougar may elicit the same response. Cougars hunt for deer, their primary prey, at dawn and dusk. They usually avoid people. Hike with a friend if you are birding early or late at the sites where these animals are mentioned.

Vehicle break-ins are possible anywhere, but they are more common at a few of the sites listed and are indicated under "Special Considerations and Hazards." Lock your car and take your valuables with you at all locations.

Please respect private property and close all gates you open. Be a courteous birder. (See the ethics guidelines in chapter 9.)

Public Transportation

Visiting several of the birding sites described in this guide without a car is possible by using Albuquerque's city bus transit system (sometimes referred to as ABQ Ride). Bus fares (2010) are $1.00 for adults and $0.35 for students and adults age 62+ with identification. If you need to transfer to another bus route during your journey, ask the driver for a one-day pass when boarding to avoid being charged full fare to change routes. Paper transfers are no longer issued. Multiple-day discount passes are also available. Bus routes, schedules, and maps are available at www.cabq.gov/transit/routes-and-schedules.

Albuquerque city bus routes provide service through most of the day. Exact times vary, but most of these routes operate between about 6:00 A.M. and 6:00 P.M., and some run later. Local routes have stops about every two blocks. Some route schedules vary throughout the day. Check the route schedule for exact times.

Note that some Albuquerque bus routes do not run at all on weekends. Those that do run usually have different schedules than on weekdays. For routes that do run on weekends, the schedule is generally different on both Saturday and Sunday.

Many bus routes that pass near the birding sites in this guide are only a commuter service. These buses run only in the morning and afternoon at rush hours. Route times vary, but most of these routes operate between about 6:00 and 9:00 A.M., and again between about 4:00 and 6:00 P.M. Buses on commuter routes make fewer stops than on other routes and only at stops marked with a red "**Commuter**" sign. It would be possible to use these routes to some of the birding sites on a weekday morning, but you would not be able to catch a return ride until late afternoon.

The following sites are within a reasonable walking distance from a city bus stop.

Along the Rio Grande Sites

Rio Grande Nature Center State Park: Bus 36 stops at Rio Grande Boulevard and Candelaria Road NW, where it is a 0.5-mile walk to the park entrance.

Albuquerque Open Space Visitor Center: Bus 155 stops at Coors Boulevard and Bosque Meadows Road NW, where it is a 0.5-mile walk to the visitor center. Bus 155 also stops at Coors and La Orilla Road NW, where you can walk 0.5 mile to the bosque trails when the Visitor Center is closed.

Sandia Foothills Sites

Embudito Canyon and Open Space: Bus 5 stops at the intersection of Tramway and Montgomery Boulevards NE at the City of Albuquerque Park and Ride. It is a 1-mile walk to the trailhead.

Embudo Canyon and Open Space: Bus 11 stops at the intersection of Lomas Boulevard and Turner Drive NE (Monday–Saturday). It is a 1.1-mile walk to the trailhead. The bus stops at Lomas and Tramway Boulevards NE on Sunday; the walk to the trailhead is 0.5 mile longer.

Copper Trailhead Open Space: Bus 11 stops at Copper Avenue NE and Turner Drive NE. It is a 0.3-mile walk to the trailhead.

Petroglyph National Monument Site

Piedras Marcadas: Bus 157 stops at Paseo del Norte and Golf Course Road NW. Walk north on Golf Course Road for 0.7 mile to the trailhead.

Albuquerque Open Space Visitor Center

On the first Sunday of each month, the Open Space sponsors guided nature walks. Call the Visitor Center at 505-897-8831 for registration and times. Space is limited. The Visitor Center posts a sightings board and a bird list. For more information, visit its Web site: www.cabq.gov/openspace/visitorcenter.html.

Bosque del Apache National Wildlife Refuge

The Friends of the Bosque del Apache operate a nature store, offer a variety of educational activities, publish a newsletter about the refuge and its activities, and sponsor the annual Festival of the Cranes. For more information, visit their Web site: www.friendsofthebosque.org.

Central New Mexico Audubon Society (CNMAS)

CNMAS is a local chapter of the National Audubon Society. The organization has monthly meetings and sponsors field trips as well as research and conservation efforts. For information on these activities, visit the CNMAS Web site: http://newmexicoaudubon.org/cnmas.

Cibola National Forest (Sandia Ranger District)

The U.S. Forest Service sponsors Tuesday-morning bird walks to locations in the Sandia and Manzano Mountains from May through mid-October. The specific locations are not scheduled in advance. Call 505-281-3304 for more information. Its publications include *Birds of the Sandia and Manzanita Mountains*, available online at www.rosyfinch.com/manzano.html or at the Sandia Ranger District Visitor Center.

eBird

Although not a strictly local resource, this Internet portal provides current information on birding "Hotspots" in each state. eBird describes Hotspots as "public birding locations created by eBird users. Using Hotspots, multiple birders can enter data into the same shared location, creating aggregated results available through 'View and Explore Data.'" For an in-depth explanation of how eBird works and how to enter data, please refer to the eBird Web site: www. ebird.org/content/ebird/about. Each site description in this guide indicates whether it is an eBird Hotspot to enable you to check current sightings before your visit. To locate the existing Hotspot, go to "Submit Observation" and enter the state and county, which will direct you to a map. Existing Hotspots have a red marker. When you click on the marker, the name will appear under "Location Name." The Hotspot name may vary slightly from the official name used in this guide. Please consider entering your own data to existing Hotspot locations.

New Mexico Ornithological Society (NMOS)

NMOS serves as the primary clearinghouse for information on the distribution, occurrence, and status of New Mexico birds. Information on rare bird sightings is summarized and published on its Web site twice a week: www.nmbirds.org. The organization's publication, *NMOS Field Notes,* is published quarterly for its members and provides a seasonal overview of the changing patterns of New Mexico's birdlife, including unusual records, breeding and wintering range changes, and changes in seasonal occurrence and migration patterns. The *NMOS Bulletin,* published four times a year, includes articles of scientific merit concerning the distribution, abundance, status, behavior, and ecology of the avifauna of New Mexico and its contiguous regions and news of interest to the New Mexico ornithological community.

NMOS sponsors the Rare Bird Alert Hotline, which compiles sightings and posts them on its Web site twice a week. The report is also posted at www.birder.com/birding/alert/index.html and on the Arizona / New Mexico list at www.birdingonthe.net. Report unusual sightings to Matt J. Baumann, compiler, at 505-264-1052 or mb687@yahoo.com.

The organization also sponsors the New Mexico Bird Records Committee, which maintains the official list of New Mexico birds. The committee requests documentation of all New Mexico records of species not currently on the official State List. A copy of the reporting form follows this section.

Rio Grande Nature Center State Park

The Friends of the Rio Grande Nature Center sponsors weekly bird walks on Saturday and Sunday. They hold three festivals during the year with specialized presentations. In conjunction with the New Mexico State Parks, they sponsor a variety of activities and classes for children. For more information, visit their Web site: www.rgnc.org.

Salinas Pueblo Missions National Monument–Quarai Unit

The National Park Service and U.S. Forest Service collaborate to sponsor activities for International Migratory Bird Day on the second Saturday in May. For information about specific activities on that day, consult their Web site: www.nps.gov/sapu/naturescience/birds.htm. The shop in the Visitor Center also carries books about birds and other wildlife.

For updates on individual sites, see: www.birdinghotspotscentralnm.com

New Mexico Rare/Unusual Bird Report

This form is intended as a guide in reporting observations of unusual birds. It may be used flexibly and need not be used at all. Leave blank any details not observed. Attach additional sheets if necessary. Attach any photographic, video recordings, or other documentation and send to

Dr. Sartor O. Williams III
New Mexico Bird Records Committee
1819 Meadowview Dr. NW
Albuquerque, NM 87104-2511
or sunbittern@earthlink.net.

Reporter (include middle initial, address, and e-mail) _____

Other observers who also identified bird _____

Date(s)/times(s) when seen _____ Locality _____

Common or scientific name _____ Number/Age/Sex_____

Habitat _____

Conditions (weather, lighting) _____

Duration _____ Optical equipment (type, power, condition)

Distance to bird _____ Size and shape _____

Behavior (flying, feeding, resting) _____

Description of what was seen (total length, body bulk, bill, eye, leg characteristics color, pattern of plumage) _____

_____

_____

Was it photographed? _____ By whom? _____ Attached? _____

Voice _____ Previous experience with species _____

Basis for identification _____

Aids (book, other birders, illustrations) _____

Positive of identification? _____ If not, explain _____

Description written: from notes made during observation _____ notes made after observation _____

Signature of reporter _____ Date/time written _____

This request for documentation should not be considered an affront but an effort to substantiate a record by obtaining concrete evidence that may be permanently preserved for all to evaluate.

CHAPTER 3

Along the Rio Grande

Albuquerque and Corrales

General Overview

The Rio Grande, New Mexico's major river, stretches about 2,000 miles from southern Colorado to the Gulf of Mexico. The region where the river flows through central New Mexico is referred to as the middle Rio Grande valley. Though the Rio Grande runs along a valley, the river did not carve the depression it follows. It flowed into a basin caused by rifting of the earth's crust. The area on either side of the river is a middle riparian woodlands, referred to as a *bosque* (Spanish for "woodlands").

The Middle Rio Grande Endangered Species Collaborative Program in central New Mexico has been working to restore habitat along the river. Artificial channels have been built at several points through the bosque to create habitat during spring runoff for the endangered Rio Grande silvery minnow to spawn and encourage habitat for the endangered Willow ("Southwestern") Flycatcher.

Propagation of the bosque's principal tree, the Rio Grande cottonwood, depends upon moisture from seasonal flooding. Though dams, levees, and flood-control measures have benefited agriculture and mitigated the impact of flooding on cities, they have prevented the germination of new cottonwoods. This changed habitat also has allowed the spread of invasive species, such as salt cedar (tamarisk). Native and introduced trees form the understory, including New Mexico and introduced Russian olive and coyote willow. Along the floor of the bosque are a variety of grasses, wildflowers, and cacti.

The bosque supports a variety of year-round and seasonal birds and is on the part of the Central Flyway that flows down through the Rocky Mountains and Rio Grande. Although there are a number of access points to the river and the adjacent riparian areas, this guide features four sites favored by local birders.

Directions to the sites along the Rio Grande can be found in the individual site descriptions.

Rio Grande Nature Center State Park

DESCRIPTION

The 170-acre Rio Grande Nature Center State Park at the west end of Candelaria Road NW in Albuquerque is surrounded by towering cottonwoods and bordered by the Rio Grande. Located on the Central Flyway, it is at an altitude of 4,500 feet. It has a documented bird list of almost 300 species and is one of Albuquerque's gems.

The gates to the park open at 8:00 A.M., and the Visitor Center opens at 10:00 A.M. Both close each day at 5:00 P.M. Some of the park's trails can be

View from parking-lot observation blind

accessed, dawn to dusk, from the paved Paseo del Bosque Trail, which runs 16 miles from Alameda Boulevard NW to Rio Bravo Boulevard SW. There is a path (labeled "bike path") that leads to the trail from the end of Candelaria Road.

Begin your visit at the blind at the east end of the parking lot, with observation openings at various heights. From the blind you can easily view resident and seasonal waterfowl in the Candelaria Wetlands. Be sure to look into the agricultural fields on your right beyond the pond for birds that forage there.

At the west end of the parking lot, take the main path (next to the bench) that leads toward the Visitor Center. Scan the trees and bushes on either side of the trail. Another bench along the trail provides a good vantage point for seasonally stocked feeders. You might want to stop to pick up a map and check out the sightings board, located just behind the main desk inside the Visitor Center.

It is worth spending some time in the glass-walled observation room that overlooks the main pond. Search the willows and Russian olives along the left side of the pond, particularly during migration, where eastern migrants sometimes have found a temporary haven. Leave the Visitor Center from the door just beyond the well-supplied nature shop. Another blind will enable you to look at both the pond and the winter-stocked feeder, which often attracts different birds than the feeder along the main path.

Rejoin the main trail, turning to your right and out the gate, and then cross the bridge. Examine the overhanging Russian olive trees growing by the water in the drainage ditch, and then either ascend the stairs or inclined path to the Paseo del Bosque Trail. Look both ways for bicyclists before crossing over the trail to the middle-elevation riparian area of the Rio Grande Nature Center State Park. You can walk any of three trails in the bosque: River Walk, Bosque Loop, or the Aldo Leopold Trail (a paved and wheelchair-accessible path), followed by the Aldo Leopold Forest Trail (not wheelchair accessible) that starts at the end of the paved loop and travels through the bosque an additional 0.5 mile.

As you wander through the bosque, be sure to look up for roosting owls or nesting Cooper's Hawks, as well as check the bushes on either side of the trail. The River Walk and Bosque Loop Trails both lead to the river; the paved path stops short of the river. When you arrive at the Rio Grande, you may find waterfowl out on the sandbars.

When you return to the main part of the park, take the first trail to the right and walk through the Wildlife Plant Garden (Main Garden). There are several benches and seasonal feeders.

Trained volunteer naturalists lead bird walks on Saturday and Sunday mornings year-round that include areas normally not open to the public, plus the opportunity (early August through the first Saturday in November and again on Saturdays mid-January through the end of March) to meet and view the activities of one of the bird banders. Since starting times vary throughout the year, call 505-344-7240 for information about the walks.

County: Bernalillo

eBird Hotspot: Rio Grande Nature Center—Candelaria Wetlands (area around the wetlands off the parking lot) and Rio Grande Nature Center (covering the rest of the park)

Web site for more information: www.rgnc.org

TARGET BIRDS

Cackling Goose Up to 100 of these geese can be found on the parking-lot pond after about 10:00 A.M. from November through mid-March. There also are Canada Geese that normally spend the night on this pond. Most have left to forage in the fields by the time the Cackling Geese arrive mid-morning.

Wood Duck It is a resident breeder and is usually seen on the left side of the pond as you look out the windows of the Visitor Center's observation room.

Greater Roadrunner It is a resident breeder. This is one of the few places in Albuquerque where you can pretty much be guaranteed to encounter one. In fact, as you pull into the parking area, you may be greeted by one as it prances across the road and peruses the area in search of a snack (usually small reptiles).

Black-chinned Hummingbird This is the primary hummingbird residing at the Nature Center, where it breeds and buzzes in and out from one of the many nectar feeders from mid-April into early October.

Ash-throated Flycatcher It nests at the Nature Center and may use one of the nest boxes, one of which is equipped with a remote video camera that can be viewed from the Visitor Center Discovery Room. It arrives mid- to late April and leaves by the end of August.

Black and Say's Phoebes Both are year-round residents and breeders. Look for Say's Phoebe in the area just east of the parking lot. Black Phoebe may be perched on the lower willow branches in the parking-lot pond or on the branches of the Russian olive along the drainage ditch.

Bewick's Wren A resident breeder, it might be found almost any place in the park.

Spotted Towhee It also is a resident breeder. In the winter, listen for it scratching in the leaves near the feeders. During spring and summer you can find a male singing from the bushes.

White-crowned Sparrow Look for it around the feeders along the main path and in the Wildlife Plant Garden (Main Garden) from early fall until almost April.

OTHER BIRDS

Other year-round birds include Mallard, Pied-billed Grebe, an occasional Great Blue Heron, Cooper's Hawk, American Kestrel, American Coot, Mourning and White-winged Doves, Western Screech-Owl, Downy Woodpecker, Belted Kingfisher, Northern Flicker, Killdeer, Black-capped Chickadee, White-breasted Nuthatch, American Robin, Red-winged Blackbird, Great-tailed Grackle, House Finch, and Lesser Goldfinch. Great Horned Owl lives in the bosque year-round but is more easily seen in early spring when the female is sitting on her nest. Ring-necked Pheasant often can be glimpsed year-round in the field beyond the parking-lot pond, and Eastern Bluebird is now a year-round resident and breeder in the riverside bosque.

A plethora of waterfowl make their winter homes in the parking-lot pond and main pond, including Gadwall, American Wigeon, Northern Shoveler, Green-winged Teal, Canvasback, Redhead, Ring-necked Duck, Lesser Scaup, Bufflehead, Hooded and Common Mergansers, and Ruddy Duck. Look for Northern Harrier and Sharp-shinned or Red-tailed Hawk as they course over the fields during the winter. Mountain Chickadees join the Black-capped. Sandhill Crane, Canada Goose, and occasionally Western Meadowlark and Savannah Sparrow feed in the agricultural fields beyond the parking-lot pond from mid-November to early March. Scan the edges of the ponds for Wilson's Snipe. As you walk the bosque trails during the winter, look for Ruby-crowned Kinglet, Yellow-rumped Warbler, Dark-eyed Junco, and American Goldfinch. Hermit Thrush and Song Sparrow often can be seen skulking under the willows along both ponds.

During the summer, you may find Summer Tanager, as well as Blue and Black-headed Grosbeaks as you walk on any of the bosque trails. Listen for

Common Yellowthroat and Yellow-breasted Chat. Barn, Northern Rough-winged, and Cliff Swallows swoop over the parking-lot pond, starting mid-morning from April through September. Look for Green Heron and Black-crowned Night-Heron and Snowy or Cattle Egret along the edges of one of the ponds. Spotted Sandpiper is often seen during the summer around the edges of the parking-lot pond, and Blue-winged and Cinnamon Teal are frequently spotted in the pond itself. Western Kingbird is often seen in the field next to the parking lot.

During spring and fall migration, you may spot Western Tanager, various flycatchers (Olive-sided, Western Wood-Pewee, and *Empidonax* species), and several species of western wood warblers, including Wilson's, MacGillivray's, Yellow, and Black-throated Gray. Every year eastern strays have dropped in for a few days during migration. Six species of swallows can be seen over the parking-lot pond during migration: Bank, Barn, Cliff, Northern Rough-winged, Tree, and Violet-green.

DIRECTIONS

By car: From the intersection of I-25 and I-40, drive west on I-40 for 2.5 miles to Exit 157A, Rio Grande Boulevard NW. Turn right on Rio Grande Boulevard NW, and travel north approximately 1.5 miles. At Candelaria Road NW, turn left for about 0.5 mile to the end of the street and the park entrance.

Public transportation: City bus 36 stops at Rio Grande Boulevard NW and Candelaria Road NW (a 0.5-mile walk to the nature center).

PARKING

The parking lot is open daily 8:00 A.M.–5:00 P.M. Gates are locked at 5:00 P.M.

FEES

Daily fee is currently $3.00 per vehicle. The following passes can be used in lieu of the fee: Friends of the Rio Grande Nature Center member's parking pass; New Mexico State Parks day-use or camping permit.

SPECIAL CONSIDERATIONS AND HAZARDS

- Pets and bicycles: They are not allowed within the park.
- Harvester ants: You may encounter these hills of stinging ants on or adjacent to any of the trails.

- Mosquitoes: Mosquitoes may be present on the bosque trails during the summer rainy season.

- Accessibility: The Visitor Center and Aldo Leopold Trail are wheel-chair accessible. The paths within the main part of the park are packed dirt or gravel. Both the River Walk and Bosque Loop Trails are dirt and often not level. The River Walk has some stairs.
- Restrooms: Available in the Visitor Center
- Water: Drinking fountain in the Visitor Center
- Picnic tables: Picnic facilities are adjacent to the parking lot.

FOOD, GAS, AND LODGING

There are numerous restaurants and gas stations throughout Albuquerque. Lodging is concentrated at most exits along I-25 and I-40.

Albuquerque Open Space Visitor Center and Bosque Trails

DESCRIPTION

The Albuquerque Open Space Visitor Center, located along the west side of the Rio Grande and adjacent to 24 acres of agricultural fields, provides visitors with an opportunity to view birds in a variety of habitats. The fields are planted seasonally and staggered so that seed can become available at various times. A rooftop viewing platform provides a unique opportunity to observe wintering Sandhill Cranes. A marsh, on your left as you enter the Open Space, attracts a variety of birds.

The Visitor Center, open Tuesday through Sunday 9:00 A.M.–5:00 P.M., offers an assortment of activities, including informative displays and a monthly nature walk (information is on the Web site, or call 505-897-8831). After perusing the Visitor Center and picking up a trail map, head back outside and look for the sign on the west side of the parking lot designating access to the 0.25-mile path that leads to the bosque trails.

If you want to explore the bosque when the Visitor Center is closed, you can park behind the church a short distance south on Coors Boulevard NW (see directions under "Parking").

Regardless of where you park, the path to the bosque trails crosses the Riverside Drain. At this point, you can walk along the levee or head into the bosque. The trail into the bosque forks after a short distance. The trail to the

Entrance to Visitor Center

left (Canopy Loop Trail) wanders through the woods for about a mile and then joins the River Loop Trail. If you keep walking straight ahead, the trail leads to the river.

The path along the levee may be a good place to explore during the winter or early spring when the branches of the cottonwood trees are bare, since it provides a better vantage point to look for a raptor nest or porcupine.

As you walk along the paths within the bosque, check the shrubs on either side of the trail and look up to scan the larger branches. There are several sandbars across from the River Loop Trail access where waterfowl often rest.

County: Bernalillo
eBird Hotspot: No
Web site: www.cabq.gov/openspace/visitorcenter.html

Sandhill Crane The Visitor Center arranges for crops to be planted to provide food for wintering Sandhill Cranes, which are in residence from October through February. Various viewing areas are set up to enhance the visitor's opportunity to observe cranes foraging in the fields. One or more might also be found resting on a sandbar seen from the River Loop Trail.

Greater Roadrunner Spotting a Greater Roadrunner is highly likely along either of the bosque trails.

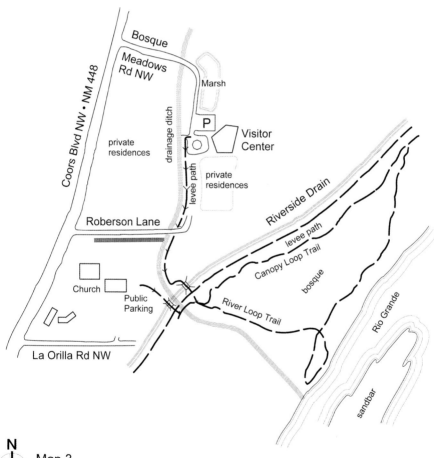

N

Map 3
Albuquerque Open Space Visitor Center & Bosque Trails

Black and Say's Phoebes Both are year-round residents and breeders. Look for Black Phoebe along the drain and Say's Phoebe near the agricultural fields or on the bosque trails.

Western Bluebird It is present fall through spring in the area of the bosque trails.

OTHER BIRDS

Year-round birds include Canada Goose, Mallard, Wood Duck, Ring-necked Pheasant, Red-tailed and Cooper's Hawks, American Kestrel, White-winged and Mourning Doves, Downy Woodpecker, Northern Flicker, American Crow, Western Scrub-Jay, Black-capped Chickadee, Bushtit, White-breasted Nuthatch, American Robin, Spotted Towhee, Red-winged Blackbird, Great-tailed Grackle, House Finch, and Lesser Goldfinch. Other year-round possibilities include Great Blue Heron, Black-crowned Night-Heron, Killdeer, Western Screech-Owl, Great Horned Owl, Belted Kingfisher, Bewick's Wren, and Eastern Bluebird.

Birds that are summer residents include Cattle and Snowy Egrets; Green Heron; Turkey Vulture; Northern Rough-winged, Cliff, and Barn Swallows; Common Nighthawk; Black-chinned Hummingbird; Ash-throated Fly-catcher; Western Wood-Pewee; Western Kingbird; Common Yellowthroat; Yellow-breasted Chat; Summer Tanager; Black-headed and Blue Grosbeaks; and Bullock's Oriole.

During winter look for Northern Shoveler, American Coot, Bald Eagle, and Ring-billed Gull on or near the river. Wintering raptors include Northern Harrier. Other regular wintering species include Mountain Chickadee and Dark-eyed Junco. Additional possibilities are Ruby-crowned Kinglet, Hermit Thrush, Yellow-rumped Warbler, Song and White-crowned Sparrows, and Western Meadowlark.

During migration, White-faced Ibis may visit the marsh, and other fly-catchers, swallows, warblers, Blue-gray Gnatcatcher, and Western Tanager may be seen.

DIRECTIONS

By car: From the intersection of I-40 and I-25, travel north on I-25 to Exit 232, Paseo del Norte (NM 423). At the exit ramp, turn left on NM 423 and travel west (crossing the Rio Grande) approximately 4.5 miles. Exit at Coors Boulevard NW (NM 448), turn left, and drive south approximately 1 mile.

Watch for a large brown sign for Albuquerque Open Space Visitor Center. Turn left onto Bosque Meadows Road NW, and follow it 0.2 mile to the parking lot.

Public transportation: City bus 155 stops at Coors Boulevard NW and Bosque Meadows Road NW and at Coors and La Orilla Road NW.

PARKING

The Open Space Visitor Center has a large parking area. Public parking is also available behind a nearby church. To reach this parking lot, travel south on Coors Boulevard NW approximately 0.5 mile from Bosque Meadows Road NW to La Orilla Road NW. Turn left, and drive east to the large parking area on the left.

FEES

None

SPECIAL CONSIDERATIONS AND HAZARDS

- Harvester ants: You may encounter these hills of stinging ants on or adjacent to any of the trails.
- Mosquitoes: Mosquitoes may be bothersome on the bosque trails, especially in the early morning or evening during the summer rainy season.

FACILITIES

- Accessibility: The Visitor Center itself is fully accessible in compliance with the guidelines created under the Americans with Disabilities Act (ADA). The path to the bosque trails is wide and level. The bosque trails are single track and sometimes uneven.
- Restrooms: Available in the Visitor Center
- Water: Drinking fountain in the Visitor Center
- Picnic tables: None available

FOOD, GAS, AND LODGING

There are numerous restaurants and gas stations along Coors Boulevard NW. Lodging is concentrated at most exits along I-25 and I-40.

Alameda Bosque and Open Space

DESCRIPTION

This site is located at an elevation of approximately 5,000 feet in one of Albuquerque's Open Space areas along the Rio Grande at the north end of Albuquerque. The area offers a variety of habitats, including a wetland, drainage-ditch vegetation, middle-elevation riparian cottonwood forest, and river sandbars.

Turn left out of the parking lot and walk a short way along the paved, multiuse Paseo del Bosque Trail. Start your exploration by walking partially around the area referred to as the Alameda Wetlands, an area collaboratively constructed to replicate the natural wetlands that existed historically in the Rio Grande's floodplain. This will be most productive during the winter when you can get glimpses of the water after the willow leaves fall. During the remainder of the year, growth of willows obscures views of the pond. There is public access only around a portion of the pond, so you will need to retrace your steps.

Turn left and walk south along the Paseo del Bosque Trail, keeping an eye out for bicyclists, until you reach a footbridge. During the winter season, sparrows often enjoy the seed heads of wildflowers and grasses along the top of the levee and alongside the water. You should be able to see songbird activity in the wildflowers and shrubs during migration. Check out the large elm trees growing just south of the bridge.

Next, cross over the drainage ditch, and then head up and over the levee on a dirt service road. Follow the service road as it circles a pond, and continue over to the edge of the river next to the mustard-colored building, Albuquerque Bernalillo County Water Utility Authority's industrial water-recycling project. The paved walkway around the building provides access to excellent views of the river.

The river is deeper at this location during the winter, which provides a good vantage point for Common Merganser and other waterfowl. Retrace your steps along the service road to the drain. Walk along the west side of the drainage ditch and under Alameda Boulevard until you reach the paved bike trail.

Walk down to the picnic area, and then take the unmarked trail that heads north through the bosque. There will be a variety of seasonal birds and several vantage points where you can look out at the river. This area can at times be rich with migrating sparrows and warblers. After about 0.5 mile, look for a trail that leads out of the bosque and up onto the levee.

Once on the levee, walk south to the paved trail, scanning into the bosque, along the drain, and into the trees that border the residential neighborhood that backs up to the area.

At the paved trail, head west across the old Alameda Bridge (now a multiuse trail).The sandbar vegetation below the bridge often harbors a variety of birds, including stray sparrows during the winter and warblers during migration. In the spring you may even see a Canada Goose on her nest.

From the middle of the bridge you will have a good view of the sandbars where wintering gulls congregate. Scan the vegetation on the west side of the river, as Black-crowned Night-Heron often can be seen. Follow the paved path, crossing over the footbridge and under the new bridge to return to the parking lot.

View from old Alameda Bridge during Albuquerque International Balloon Fiesta

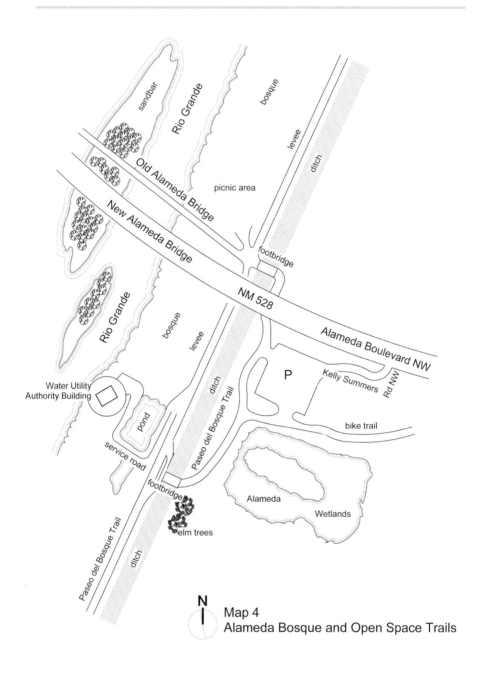

sandbar

Rio Grande

bosque

Old Alameda Bridge

levee

ditch

picnic area

New Alameda Bridge

footbridge

NM 528

Alameda Boulevard NW

Rio Grande

bosque

levee

ditch

P

Kelly Summers

Rd NW

Water Utility
Authority Building

pond

Paseo del Bosque Trail

bike trail

service road

footbridge

Alameda
Wetlands

elm trees

Paseo del Bosque Trail

ditch

N

Map 4
Alameda Bosque and Open Space Trails

County: Bernalillo
eBird **Hotspot:** Alameda Bridge

TARGET BIRDS

Common Merganser Look for it on the river. The best place to spot one is from the area behind the industrial water-recycling project's building.

Bald Eagle One or two Bald Eagles winter (December and January) along the Rio Grande and often can be seen during flight or perched in one of the cottonwoods.

Ring-billed Gull Flocks of several hundred Ring-billed Gulls make their winter home on this section of the Rio Grande. You can see them best from the middle of the old bridge. Check the flocks carefully, especially during January and February, since almost every winter a stray species of gull will be mixed in. These sightings are usually reported on the rare bird alert (RBA). (See the section on the NMOS RBA Hotline in chapter 2 under "Local Birding Information and Resources.")

Cliff Swallow Rows of nests are visible most years under the new Alameda Bridge from about mid-May to mid-July. They are best viewed from the old bridge. Look for flights of swallows rebuilding their nests or feeding their young.

Bewick's Wren It breeds in the area and can be seen year-round.

Common Yellowthroat This warbler breeds in the dense foliage along the river. While normally only a summer resident along the Rio Grande in New Mexico, it occasionally has been seen during the winter months. Often it is difficult to see, but its distinctive song announces its presence.

Summer Tanager It breeds in the cottonwood trees in the bosque.

Blue Grosbeak It is common in the summer. Listen for its metallic *chink* call coming from the thickets.

OTHER BIRDS

Birds that can be seen year-round include Canada Goose, Wood Duck, Gadwall (more frequently in winter), Mallard, Black-crowned Night-Heron, Cooper's Hawk, American Coot, Greater Roadrunner, Belted Kingfisher, Downy and Hairy Woodpeckers, Northern Flicker, Black and Say's Phoebes, American Crow, Black-capped Chickadee (more frequently in winter), Bushtit, White-breasted Nuthatch, American Robin, Spotted Towhee, Lesser Goldfinch, and House Finch.

During the winter months you can expect to see American Wigeon, Northern Shoveler, Ring-necked Duck, Sandhill Crane, Wilson's Snipe, Ruby-crowned Kinglet, Yellow-rumped Warbler (both "Audubon's and "Myrtle"), Song and White-crowned Sparrows, Dark-eyed Junco, and American Goldfinch. Since a White-throated Sparrow sometimes can be seen in a flock of White-crowned Sparrows, be sure to check each bird in a flock if this bird is of interest to you. This site often attracts stray sparrows during the winter, which are reported on the New Mexico RBA.

Summer residents and breeders include Cooper's Hawk, Black-chinned Hummingbird, Ash-throated Flycatcher, Western Kingbird, Yellow-breasted Chat, and Black-headed Grosbeak. Snowy Egret often can be glimpsed along the river.

During their migration, you can expect to see White-faced Ibis, Rufous Hummingbird (fall only), Violet-green and Northern Rough-winged Swallows, Western Tanager, Wilson's Warbler (and other less abundant migrating western warblers), and Chipping Sparrow. During early November and late February, look overhead to watch the large flocks of Sandhill Cranes as they migrate to and from their wintering grounds in New Mexico; you will hear their distinctive call to alert you to their presence.

DIRECTIONS

By car: From the intersection of I-25 and I-40 in Albuquerque, drive north on I-25 approximately 5.5 miles to Exit 233, Alameda Boulevard NW (NM 528). Turn left (west) on Alameda Boulevard NW (NM 528), and drive approximately 3.3 miles. Turn left (just before Alameda crosses the Rio Grande) onto Kelly Summers Road NW to enter the Alameda Open Space parking lot.

Public transportation: None available

PARKING

There is a large parking lot with ample parking.

FEES

None

- Harvester ants: Before standing still to look at a bird, look down to make sure you are not standing on an anthill.
- Mosquitoes: You might encounter mosquitoes in the bosque during the summer rainy season.

FACILITIES

- Accessibility: The paved Paseo del Bosque Trail and the old Alameda Bridge are wheelchair accessible.
- Restrooms: Two are wheelchair accessible but located in a part of the parking lot with a rough surface.
- Water: None available
- Picnic tables: There are several picnic tables in the bosque adjacent to the old bridge over the river.

FOOD, GAS, AND LODGING

Numerous restaurants and gas stations are available on the west side of the Rio Grande. Drive west on Alameda Boulevard NW (NM 528), and cross the new Alameda Bridge to Coors Boulevard NW / Corrales Road (NM 448). Lodging is concentrated at most exits along I-25 and I-40.

Corrales Bosque

DESCRIPTION

The area along the Rio Grande in the north part of the Village of Corrales, just north of Albuquerque, provides a diversity of habitats offering excellent birding at all times of the year. There are two main access points used by birders—at the end of Romero Road and farther north at the Rio Rancho Bosque Preserve, referred to by local birders as the North Corrales Bosque. Each access location is described separately.

Romero Road: This is an unpaved road that leads alongside several rural farms, some with fruit trees. You can walk along a path that heads south on the west side of the irrigation ditch and provides a good view of the fruit trees. There is a barricade at the end of Romero Road to prevent non-service vehicles from driving up on the levee. Walk around and start by checking out the irrigation ditch on either side. You can then either walk north along the compacted earth levee or along the edge of the channel. There is always a lot of bird activity, not only in the willows and Russian

Birders along the drainage ditch on Romero Road at Corrales Bosque

olive trees along the banks but also in the larger trees that screen the private residences beyond, as well as on the bosque side of the levee. After about 0.5 mile the levee ends at a diversion channel that runs into the Rio Grande. Walk along the broad, open channel toward the river. The row of willows and Russian olives along a side channel of the river are often active with birds. Backtrack slightly and head into the bosque on an uneven, single-track trail. Large cottonwood trees dominate the upper story, with a variety of smaller trees growing underneath. As you walk through the woods, check and listen for bird activity in the tops of the trees, as well as in the understory. After walking about 0.5 mile, you will reach an access point where you can view the river and the trees on the far side. A trail leads back to the levee. You will exit the bosque near Romero Road. To reach the other access point, you will need to drive back to Corrales Road, turn right, and travel north for 0.9 mile to the turnoff.

North Corrales Bosque: The access point to the North Corrales Bosque is at the end of a dirt road, bordered on the left by a community park and on the right by a housing development. Dirt roads run along both sides of the irrigation ditch. You can drive on either one. Watch for deep ruts near the entrance and along the road into the parking area, which can be difficult to maneuver following a rain.

From the parking area, first walk along a narrow trail that heads north along the edge of a bluff overlooking the Rio Grande. This location provides excellent views up and down the river. After returning to the parking area, head into the bosque on an uneven single-track trail that leads south through towering cottonwood trees and bushy understory. Follow the trail through the middle-elevation riparian bosque for about 0.5 mile until you see a path that leads up to the levee. Follow the levee north to the parking area, checking the trees and understory in the bosque from a different vantage point, as well as perusing the drainage ditch and trees in the residential area beyond.

County: Sandoval

eBird Hotspots: Corrales-Romero Road and Corrales-Northernmost

TARGET BIRDS

Great Horned Owl It is a year-round resident and nests in the bosque. It can most easily be spotted before the cottonwoods leaf out and when it is nesting mid-March through April. Search the large cottonwood limbs, where it may be roosting silently. Porcupines often can be seen here as well. Walking along the dike provides a particularly good vantage point.

Belted Kingfisher Look for the kingfisher either above the irrigation ditch north of Romero Road or on a limb over the river.

Black Phoebe This phoebe is a year-round resident and breeder. It almost always can be seen on one of the branches overhanging the irrigation ditch north of Romero Road.

Yellow-breasted Chat It breeds in the willows along the river. Listen for its chatter as you walk along the trail through the bosque at either location to help you locate where it is perched.

Summer Tanager It nests in the bosque or in the tall trees on the property backing up to the irrigation ditch north of Romero Road. You may catch a glimpse of one from late April through September.

Black-headed Grosbeak It is a summer resident. Check for it in the bosque from late April through mid-September at both locations, as well as in the tall trees on the property adjacent to the irrigation ditch north of Romero Road.

Blue Grosbeak This species of grosbeak is also a summer resident. It is most easily spotted in the orchard and plant nursery just south of the Romero Road parking area from May until early October.

Lazuli Bunting Although the Lazuli Bunting is seen only reliably during spring (May) and fall (September) migrations, Corrales Bosque is one of the dependable places to view this species in the Albuquerque area. Look for it along the back side of the residential area at the North Corrales location.

OTHER BIRDS

At any time of the year, you may find Canada Goose, Mallard, Great Blue Heron, Cooper's Hawk, Downy Woodpecker, Northern Flicker, Say's Phoebe, American Robin, Black-capped Chickadee, Bushtit, White-breasted Nuthatch, Bewick's Wren, Red-winged Blackbird, and House Finch.

During the winter, scan the river for a variety of wintering waterfowl, including American Wigeon, Green-winged Teal, and Common Merganser. Although the vantage point for observing gulls is better at the Alameda Open Space (see site description), it is possible to see Ring-billed Gulls resting on one of the sandbars here. One or two Bald Eagles winter in this area and often can be observed as they fly down the river. Both "Myrtle" and "Audubon's" subspecies of the Yellow-rumped Warbler winter here, as do Ruby-crowned Kinglet, Mountain Chickadee, Hermit Thrush, Song and White-crowned Sparrows, Dark-eyed Junco, and Lesser and American Goldfinches.

Summer residents and breeders include Ash-throated Flycatcher, Western Wood-Pewee, Black-chinned Hummingbird, Barn Swallow, Yellow Warbler, and Common Yellowthroat.

A variety of warblers are spotted frequently during both spring and fall migrations, including Orange-crowned, Virginia's, MacGillivray's, and Wilson's. Among other species seen during both spring and fall migrations are Violet-green, Northern Rough-winged, Bank, and Cliff Swallows; Plumbeous and Warbling Vireos; Gray Catbird; Western Tanager; and Chipping Sparrow and other sparrows. A variety of *Empidonax* flycatchers migrate through the bosque. Dusky Flycatcher is most frequent.

By car: From the intersection of I-25 and I-40 in Albuquerque, drive north on I-25 approximately 5.5 miles to Exit 223, Alameda Boulevard NW (NM 528). Turn left (west) on Alameda Boulevard NW (NM 528), and travel approximately 4 miles (crossing the Rio Grande) to Corrales Road (NM 448). Turn right (north) on Corrales Road, and drive through the Village of Corrales for approximately 5 miles. The village is serious about enforcing its posted speed limits. Romero Road will be on your right (a greater than 90-degree turn). There is a yellow horse-and-rider sign that is easier to see than the street sign. Follow the dirt road for 0.2 mile to its end.

The North Corrales site is 0.9 mile farther north just opposite Paseo Cesar Chavez. Make a sharp right turn just before the Rio Rancho city limits sign, and follow the dirt road into the parking area.

Public transportation: None in the Village of Corrales

PARKING

There is a small dirt parking area at the end of Romero Road. If that is full, you can parallel park along the north side of the road.

There is a larger dirt parking area at the North Corrales location.

FEES

None

SPECIAL CONSIDERATIONS AND HAZARDS

- Harvester ants: You may encounter these hills of stinging ants on or adjacent to any of the trails. Before standing still to view a bird, look down to make sure you are not standing on an anthill.
- Mosquitoes: You might encounter mosquitoes on the bosque trails during the summer rainy season.
- Driving hazard: After heavy rains, the dirt road to the North Corrales site may be impassable by all except four-wheel drive/high-clearance vehicles.

FACILITIES

- Accessibility: Neither area is wheelchair accessible.
- Restrooms: None available. The closest restrooms to Romero Road are at the gas station mini-marts at the south end of Corrales. There

is a mini-mart 0.7 mile northwest of the North Corrales site at the intersection of Corrales Road (NM 448) and Pat D'Arco Highway (NM 528).

- Water: None available
- Picnic tables: There is a picnic table in the Rio Rancho city park along the dirt road into the North Corrales site.

FOOD, GAS, AND LODGING

Restaurants, small cafés, and bed-and-breakfast-style lodging are located 1.5 to 2 miles south of Romero Road on Corrales Road (NM 448) clustered in the central area of the Village of Corrales. The nearest hotel can be reached by traveling approximately 2 miles northwest of Romero Road on Corrales Road, then left (south) on Rio Rancho Boulevard (NM 528) for 1 mile to Northern Boulevard. The nearest gas station is at the south end of the Village of Corrales as well as at the intersection of NM 448 and NM 528. NM 528 and NM 448 intersect twice: at the north end (in Rio Rancho) of the Village of Corrales, and on the south end (in Albuquerque).

CHAPTER 4

Sandia Foothills

General Overview

Five of the described sites in the Sandia Foothills are located along the base of the west face of the Sandia Mountains, primarily in the major drainage canyons. Three Gun Spring and access to HawkWatch are in the south-facing foothills along Tijeras Pass. Several canyons have springs formed from water runoff that has seeped between rock layers and provides mini-riparian habitats within the canyons. The rest of the landscape is desert scrub and grassland, transitioning to piñon-juniper woodlands as each canyon rises in elevation.

Most of the area at the base of the foothills is part of Albuquerque's Open Space. Each site has trails that lead to the Sandia Mountain Wilderness, which is under the jurisdiction of Cibola National Forest.

General Directions

From the intersection of I-25 and I-40 in Albuquerque, travel east approximately 7.5 miles on I-40 to Exit 167. Take Tramway Boulevard NE (NM 556) north. All sites in this section may be accessed from Tramway Boulevard NE except Three Gun Spring (refer to the individual site description for directions).

Elena Gallegos Picnic Area

DESCRIPTION

The Elena Gallegos Picnic Area is a 640-acre developed section of the Sandia Foothills that is part of Albuquerque's Open Space. Starting at an elevation

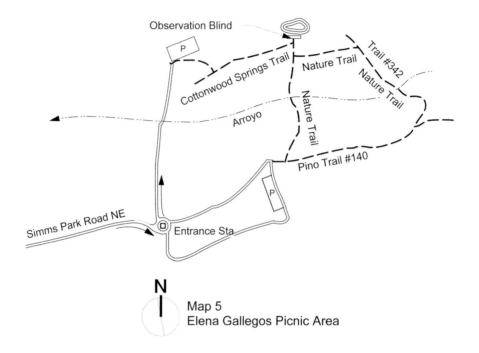

Observation Blind

P

Cottonwood Springs Trail

Nature Trail

Trail #342

Nature Trail

Arroyo

Nature Trail

Pino Trail #140

P

Simms Park Road NE

Entrance Sta.

N

Map 5
Elena Gallegos Picnic Area

of 6,500 feet, this area is more a piñon-juniper habitat than the desert scrub that characterizes most of the other foothills locations in this guide. The landscape is dotted with one-seed junipers and piñon pines, in addition to foothills scrub plants. A stand of scrub oak can be found in the arroyo on the Nature Trail. Many bird species here overlap with those found at the other foothills sites described in this guide, but this area attracts some additional species.

If you turn left just past the entrance station, the road leads past a group reservation area to the Cottonwood Springs Trailhead. This wheelchair-accessible 0.23-mile paved trail, which is on the north boundary of the park, ascends to a pond and wildlife blind. The pond (a former stock pond) at the blind is small and deep and, with the exception of an occasional Mallard, does not appeal to waterbirds; however, the trees surrounding the pond attract several species of birds at all times of the year. No bicycles are allowed on this trail, which allows for leisurely walking and bird observation.

Exiting the blind, continue straight ahead for 0.22 mile on the Nature Trail (not wheelchair accessible) that descends through a small arroyo and ends at the south parking area. Follow the Pino Trail (#140) from the trailhead at this parking area, and continue 0.25 mile until it intersects with the Nature Trail, which is also labeled Trail #342. Turn left and continue about 0.2 mile until you arrive at the first trail on your left (the sign will point to the continuation of the Nature Trail). The section of the Nature Trail that overlaps with Trail #342 is rutted, as well as heavily used by mountain bikers, so it is best to walk near the edge of the trail, stepping off the trail if you stop to look at a bird. Turn left from #342 onto the Nature Trail, and follow it until you turn right toward the blind. You will now be back on the Cottonwood Springs Trail; follow it back to the trailhead parking.

The area is open 7:00 A.M. until 9:00 P.M. during the summer months (April–September) and 7:00 A.M. until 7:00 P.M. the remainder of the year.

Blind along Cottonwood Springs Trail

County: Bernalillo
eBird Hotspot: Elena Gallegos Picnic Area

TARGET BIRDS

Scaled and Gambel's Quail Both quail are year-round residents but not as wide-spread as they are at other sites along the Sandia Foothills. Listen for them calling in the late spring and early summer before they start nesting. During winter, you might happen upon a covey of quail as they scurry across the trail.

Juniper Titmouse This small bird is glimpsed most frequently at all times of the year as it scrounges for insects in the dense foliage of junipers and piñon pines. You may hear its call notes as it works the branches. It is usually seen in the company of another titmouse.

Western Bluebird This bluebird is present from mid-September through mid-March. It is easily seen perched on top of the conifers or foraging in the branches, where it might look like a tree ornament.

Townsend's Solitaire This species is an altitudinal migrator that arrives in the fall and stays through March, when it leaves for higher elevations. You may see one perched alone in a conifer or in the bare branches of the trees near the blind.

OTHER BIRDS

At any time of the year, you can find flocks of Bushtits busy in the pines and junipers. Canyon Towhee and Northern Flicker are prevalent. Spotted Towhee can be found along Trail #342. Bewick's Wren is another plentiful year-round bird. Western Scrub-Jay sails between evergreens. American Robin and House Finch are also plentiful, especially along the Cottonwood Springs Trail. This is a habitat where you might see a Ladder-backed Wood-pecker, although it is not guaranteed. Cooper's Hawk is found year-round, and both Great Horned Owl and Western Screech-Owl nest here. Greater Roadrunner is often seen along the road leading to the park.

During the summer months, you can observe Cassin's Kingbird, Black-chinned and Broad-tailed Hummingbirds, Barn Swallow, and Blue-gray Gnatcatcher.

During winter, look for Eastern Bluebird, Chipping Sparrow, Dark-eyed Junco, Cassin's Finch, and Pine Siskin.

By car: From the intersection of I-25 and I-40 in Albuquerque, travel east on I-40 approximately 8 miles. At Exit 167, go north approximately 6 miles on Tramway Boulevard NE (NM 556) to Simms Park Road NE. Look for the Elena Gallegos Picnic Area sign. The entrance station is east (right) 1 mile at the end of Simms Park Road NE.

Public transportation: Not recommended. The nearest city bus stop (route 1 at Lowell Street and Spain Road NE) is at least a 2.5-mile walk to Elena Gallegos Picnic Area.

PARKING

There is ample parking at several locations throughout the park. The parking lots open at 7:00 A.M.

FEES

The fee is $2.00 on weekends and $1.00 on weekdays (check the Web site www.cabq.gov/openspace/elenagallegos.html for current information).

SPECIAL CONSIDERATIONS AND HAZARDS

Rattlesnakes may be present during warm weather.

FACILITIES

- Accessibility: The Cottonwood Springs Trail leading to the observation blind is paved.
- Restrooms: Wheelchair-accessible restrooms are located near both the north and south parking areas.
- Water: Water is available near the picnic areas from May through September.
- Picnic tables: There are several covered picnic areas off the south parking lot (on your right as you enter the park) and two reservation areas with barbecue grills.

FOOD, GAS, AND LODGING

There are numerous restaurants and gas stations throughout Albuquerque. Lodging is concentrated at most exits along I-25 and I-40.

DESCRIPTION

This site is included here because it is the only wheelchair-accessible site with grassland-foothills scrub habitat other than the Cottonwood Springs Trail at Elena Gallegos Picnic Area. Good birding is available from the perimeter of the parking lot and along the paved sidewalk on either side of the parking area. The site is maintained by the High Desert Residential Owners Association in cooperation with the U.S. Forest Service and is open to the public between 5:00 A.M. and 9:00 P.M. (gate is locked at 9:00 P.M.).

The parking lot is planted with desert willow, cottonwood, bear grass, and piñon pine. The natural habitat on either side of the parking lot consists of chamisa (rabbit brush), Apache plume, and desert grasses and scrub.

The trail leading from the parking area continues through a wide valley and is very popular with runners and mountain bikers, thus not as quiet a location for birding as the other foothills canyons.

BIRDS

From the parking lot and adjacent paved sidewalks, you might see Say's Phoebe, Western Scrub-Jay, American Robin, and House Finch year-round. Other potential birds include Scaled and Gambel's Quail, Greater Roadrunner, Juniper Titmouse, Curve-billed Thrasher, and Canyon Towhee. In the summer, look for Black-chinned Hummingbird, particularly in the desert willows, Cassin's and Western Kingbirds on the nearby open areas, and Black-throated Sparrow; and in winter, Western Bluebird, Townsend's Solitaire, White-crowned Sparrow, and Dark-eyed Junco.

County: Bernalillo

eBird Hotspot: No

DIRECTIONS

By car: See Sandia Foothills General Overview for directions to this area. From the intersection of Tramway Boulevard NE (NM 556) and Spain Road NE, travel east 0.75 mile to the T intersection where Spain Road ends. Turn right on High Desert Place NE. The trailhead parking area will be an immediate left.

Public transportation: None available

Parking area at trailhead of Bear Canyon Open Space

PARKING

There is a small parking lot, including two designated wheelchair-accessible parking spaces.

FEES

None

SPECIAL CONSIDERATIONS AND HAZARDS

- Rattlesnakes: Be alert for rattlesnakes during warm weather.
- Harvester ants: The anthills may be located next to the sidewalk.

FACILITIES

- Restrooms: The portable toilet is not wheelchair accessible. The nearest wheelchair-accessible restrooms are in the fast-food restaurants about a mile south on the corner of Tramway and Montgomery Boulevards NE.

- ■ Water: Drinking water is available from a pump, complete with large aluminum bowl for dogs.
- ■ Picnic tables: None available

FOOD, GAS, AND LODGING

There are numerous restaurants and gas stations throughout Albuquerque. Lodging is concentrated at most exits along I-25 and I-40.

Embudito Canyon and Open Space

DESCRIPTION

The trail into Embudito Canyon lies just north of Montgomery Boulevard NE and starts at one of the Albuquerque Open Space parking areas, at an elevation of 6,200 feet. Parking places fill up early, particularly on weekends, as the Embudito Trail is popular with backpackers and hikers who climb to the crest of the Sandia Mountains.

The trail slopes down slightly as you exit the north end of the parking area. Right away, the Foothills Trail (#365) veers off to the left. Instead, continue straight ahead on Trail #192, the Embudito Canyon Trail, which almost immediately enters the Sandia Mountain Wilderness. You will approach a large stand of cholla cactus, which extends for about 100 yards.

Trail #192 has been rerouted and turns left and heads up the side of the canyon. It is not necessary to continue on Trail #192 to see the target birds. Instead, stay on the Old Trail that leads along an arroyo. The desert scrub vegetation becomes more varied, including four-wing saltbush and Apache plume. Walk about 0.25 mile until the canyon narrows and water trickles into the remnants of an old concrete livestock trough (which does not seem to attract birds). Check the bushes and trees on either side of the trail. The trail beyond this point, heading farther into the canyon, is difficult and requires scrambling over rocks; it is not necessary to go beyond this point for a profitable birding experience.

At this point you may want to follow the unmarked, but clearly discernible, portion of the Embudito Canyon Trail that heads up the side of the canyon. This part of the trail is more rugged and crosses over larger boulders, climbing quickly to an elevation of over 7,000 feet. Many hikers use a

View of valley from Embudito Canyon Trail

walking stick to prevent falls on the disintegrating granite trail surface. This side trip is certainly optional.

As you leave the parking area, drive slowly down Trailhead Road NE, scanning the residential area. The area on the right, just before Cresta del Sur Court NE, has been planted by the High Desert Residential Owners Association and often attracts a variety of birds.

County: Bernalillo

eBird Hotspot: Embudito Canyon

TARGET BIRDS

Scaled and Gambel's Quail Both quail can be found in this canyon. During breeding season they are easier to spot, since the male guards its territory from a prominent location. During other times of the year, you might catch a covey scurrying in the bushes.

Common Poorwill It has been seen in the summer at dusk near the water trough on the main trail. It more likely is heard than seen.

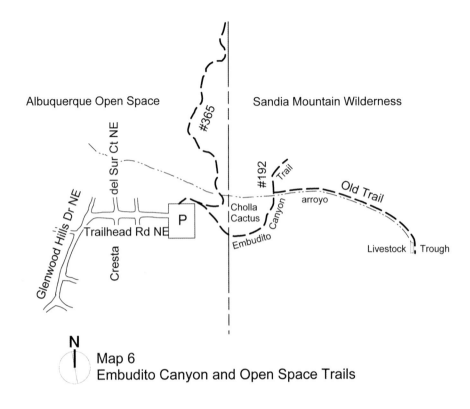

Albuquerque Open Space

Sandia Mountain Wilderness

#365

#192

Trail

Old Trail

arroyo

Cholla
Cactus

Canyon

del Sur Ct NE

Glenwood Hills Dr NE

Trailhead Rd NE

P

Embudito

Cresta

Livestock Trough

N

Map 6
Embudito Canyon and Open Space Trails

Curve-billed and Crissal Thrashers Both are year-round residents and breeders. The Curve-billed is a "can't miss" bird. Look for it in the cholla cactus. While the much less common Crissal Thrasher can also be seen on a cholla, it is just as likely to be perched on a bush, brush pile, or fence.

Black-throated, Black-chinned, and Rufous-crowned Sparrows The Black-throated Sparrow arrives in early March and stays until late fall. It is most easily observed during breeding season when the male sings from the top of Apache plume or four-wing saltbush. After breeding season, it tends to stay hidden in the bushes. Watch and listen for its activity; it often responds to pishing and will pop into view. Black-chinned Sparrow is a summer resident that arrives by late April and is gone by late September. It is not as plentiful and is more secretive. It also responds to pishing. You can easily distinguish it from the Black-throated by its facial markings and pinkish bill. It tends to prefer areas close to the edge of the canyon. You might be lucky to catch a glimpse of a Rufous-crowned Sparrow. It is a year-round resident that prefers the rocky locations at the base of the hills.

Canyon Towhee It is a prevalent year-round resident.

OTHER BIRDS

From the main trail at any time of the year, you can observe Greater Roadrunner, Western Scrub-Jay, Say's Phoebe, and House Finch. Listen for the cascading call of the Canyon Wren.

During winter months, you will find White-crowned Sparrow and Dark-eyed Junco in the bushes. Bushtits, and an occasional Northern Flicker or Ruby-crowned Kinglet, are most often encountered in the winter. While a Cooper's Hawk may be seen at any time of the year, you also might see Red-tailed Hawk in winter.

Crissal Thrasher

Black-chinned and Broad-tailed Hummingbirds and Scott's Oriole nest here throughout the summer. You might spot an occasional Rock Wren in the area of the boulders. Barn Swallows and White-throated Swifts often cruise above the canyon.

Spring migration can bring MacGillivray's Warbler and Dusky Fly-catcher. In fall migration, Rufous Hummingbird and Yellow-rumped Warbler flit in willows around the stream and among the four-wing saltbush.

DIRECTIONS

By car: From the intersection of I-25 and I-40 in Albuquerque, travel approximately 7.5 miles east on I-40 and take Exit 167. Travel north approximately 4 miles on Tramway Boulevard NE (NM-556) to Montgomery Boulevard NE, and turn right. Go east 0.5 mile, and turn left on Glenwood Hills Drive NE. Travel 0.5 mile north on Glenwood Hills Drive NE to Trailhead Road NE (sign may be obscured by foliage), which ends at the parking lot.

Public transportation: The city bus system serves the area via city bus route 5. The nearest stop is at the intersection of Tramway and Montgomery Boulevards NE. Earliest arrival time is 7:19 A.M. weekdays, 9:10 A.M. Saturday, and 9:20 A.M. Sunday. To walk to the trailhead, follow the directions under "By car" from this point. It is about 1 mile.

PARKING

The parking lot opens at 7:00 A.M. If the parking lot is full, you can park on the street, preferably a short distance downhill where there are no houses. If you go at dusk to see the Common Poorwill, park along the street, since the parking lot gate is locked at 9:00 P.M.

FEES

None

SPECIAL CONSIDERATIONS AND HAZARDS

- Rattlesnakes: Keep your eyes and ears alert for rattlesnakes during warm weather.
- Harvester ants: Their anthills abound.
- Gnats: In summer, long sleeves are recommended. Gnats are often present from midmorning until dark unless there is a strong breeze.

Desert scrub habitat along trail in winter

- Accessibility: The trails are uneven, often rutted, and sometimes narrow.
- Restrooms: None available. The closest restrooms are 1 mile away at the fast-food restaurants on the corner of Montgomery and Tramway Boulevards NE.
- Water: None available
- Picnic tables: None available

FOOD, GAS, AND LODGING

There are numerous restaurants and gas stations throughout Albuquerque. Lodging is concentrated at most exits along I-25 and I-40.

Embudo Canyon and Open Space

DESCRIPTION

Embudo Canyon is one of several canyons with hiking trails along the Sandia Foothills on the eastern edge of Albuquerque. Prickly pear and cholla cacti, four-wing saltbush, chamisa (rabbit brush), bear grass, and soapweed yucca dot the floor of the canyon, along with an occasional one-seed juniper or scrub oak, all prime perching spots for birds. In the late spring and throughout summer there are a variety of blooming wildflowers tucked between the desert scrub.

The trailhead begins at the east end of Indian School Road NE, in the Albuquerque Open Space. The fairly level main trail, #193, starts at an elevation of 6,200 feet and gradually heads toward the mountains. It is about 0.5 mile to the boundary of the Open Space and another 0.5 mile inside the wilderness area to the base of a spring. For birding purposes, there is no need to go beyond Embudo Spring, the source of a small stream at an elevation of 6,600 feet. There is a large elm tree on your right about three-quarters of the way to the spring. It can be a good place to check for warblers during migration. There is a lot of bird activity in the shrubs along the main trail, and often most of the target birds can be seen before reaching the wilderness area.

Use Trail #401, which leads north off the Indian School Road NE parking area and heads toward a distant picnic shelter beyond the power lines, to

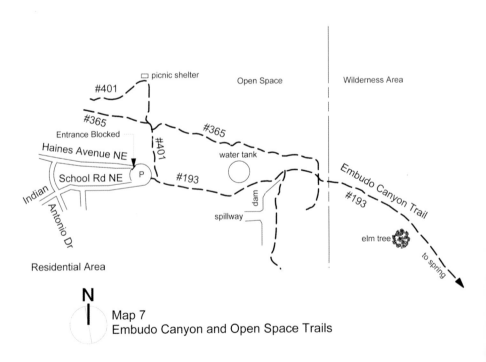

Map 7
Embudo Canyon and Open Space Trails

search areas closer to the base of the foothills. The surface of the trail consists of loose, disintegrated granite, and some sections have a steep incline. Some people prefer to use a walking stick to prevent falls.

If you have not yet seen your target birds, return to Indian School Road NE from the parking lot, turn right at the first street, Antonio Drive, and then travel to the T intersection at Haines Avenue NE. Feeders in the residential area in both directions along Haines may be productive for Gambel's and Scaled Quail. Say's Phoebe often frequents this neighborhood as well. Be sure to investigate any openings through to the Open Space and listen for quail. Retrace your route back to Indian School Road NE.

The best time to bird this area is from early to midmorning. Long sleeves are recommended to avoid distractions from gnats, which are often present in summer from sunrise until dark when there is no breeze.

This is a very popular area for hikers, mountain bikers (to the boundary of the wilderness area), and dog walkers. There is less traffic during the week.

County: Bernalillo

eBird Hotspot: Embudo Canyon

TARGET BIRDS

Scaled and Gambel's Quail Although both quail are residents, the Scaled Quail is the most prevalent in the foothill canyons. During breeding season, the male is easy to spot, perching like a sentinel over its territory. During this period, it seems to prefer sitting on one of the many large boulders. During other times of the year, you might catch one pausing on top of a four-wing saltbush or scurrying in a covey from under a bush and across a trail. At any time of the year, you will need to wander on one of the alternative trails to catch them. Another place where it may be seen easily during breeding season is from the east end of Haines Avenue NE. Gambel's Quail often can be seen near feeders along Haines.

Ladder-backed Woodpecker This species' "eat-and-run" foraging behavior makes it difficult to predict. Keep your eyes open for it on mesquite and yuccas as it hurriedly devours insects and then moves on.

Cassin's Kingbird It is a summer resident. Look for it on the power lines or in the same areas suggested for the Scott's Oriole.

Curve-billed and Crissal Thrashers They are year-round residents and breeders. They nest in and like to perch on the cholla cactus. Look for the Curve-

Gambel's Quail

billed's nest in the crooks of the cactus. The Curve-billed Thrasher is much more prevalent than the Crissal Thrasher. Listen for it as you walk along the main trail or a short distance north on Trail #401.

Cactus Wren While it is possible to see this species, it is not guaranteed. The best time to look for it is in the late winter when it is establishing its territory, when it is feeding one of its two broods, or in the early fall when it is building a roost nest. Listen for its call. It is most likely to be found near Trail #401.

Canyon Wren Often heard, this species is not always seen. You can hear its cascading call as the canyon narrows near the spring or in the small canyon just beyond and north of the shelter on Trail #401.

Black-throated, Black-chinned, and Rufous-crowned Sparrows Black-throated Sparrow is a summer resident, arriving in March. It is most easily seen during breeding season when the male sings from the top of an Apache plume or four-wing saltbush. After breeding season, it is likely concealed in the bushes. Watch and listen for its activity; it often responds to pishing and will pop into view. Black-chinned Sparrow is primarily a summer resident that arrives by the end of March and is not as common as the Black-throated. Look for it atop shrubs during breeding season. Often hidden while singing, it prefers areas closer to the base of the hills but has been seen from the main trail. Rufous-crowned Sparrow is a year-round resident and breeder that forages on the ground and under bushes, making it difficult to find. It will be seen with patience, a keen eye, and luck. It occasionally will perch on a boulder, where its plumage blends in. Check out all sparrow activity, particularly in the bushes near the large boulders at the bases of the hills.

Canyon Towhee It is common in this area where it can be seen perched on bushes or signs or foraging under the scrub.

Scott's Oriole It is a summer resident, arriving in early April and generally leaving by the end of August. It often nests in the small canyon just beyond and to the right of the picnic shelter encountered on Trail #401. The female may flush if you walk near the nest.

OTHER BIRDS

From the main trail at any time of the year, you can see Greater Roadrunner, Say's Phoebe, Western Scrub-Jay, and House Finch. Cooper's Hawk might also be seen careening across the canyon at any time of the year.

During winter months, you will find White-crowned Sparrow and Dark-eyed Junco in the bushes and sometimes sitting on the fence around the huge water storage tank. Bushtit, and an occasional Northern Flicker or Townsend's Solitaire, is most often seen during the winter. Red-tailed Hawk often can be spotted sitting on the rocks on the crests of the hills.

During the summer, Black-chinned Hummingbird nests here and Barn Swallows can be seen swooping over the grasses, primarily in the wilderness area. You might spot a Bullock's Oriole near the parking lot or an occasional Rock Wren nestled or bobbing in the boulders. Keep your eyes peeled toward the sky for the opportunity to spot White-throated Swift.

In fall migration, Rufous Hummingbird can be seen in willows around the spring-fed stream, and warblers often flit in the large elm tree on the way to the spring.

DIRECTIONS

By car: See Sandia Foothills General Overview for directions to this area. From the intersection of Tramway Boulevard NE and Indian School Road NE, travel east on Indian School Road NE 1 mile to its terminus at the Albuquerque Open Space parking area.

Public transportation: City bus 11 stops at the intersection of Lomas Boulevard and Turner Drive NE (walk uphill on Lomas Boulevard NE, which becomes Camino De La Sierra NE for 0.8 mile to Indian School Road NE. Turn right on Indian School Road NE, and walk approximately 0.3 mile to the trailhead). Monday through Friday the earliest arrival is at 6:11 A.M., and on Saturday, 6:55 A.M. Bus 11 goes only as far as Lomas and Tramway Boulevards NE on Sundays. The walk to the trailhead would be about 0.5 mile longer. See public transportation information in chapter 2.

PARKING
There is a large parking area at the Indian School Road NE trailhead. The parking area opens at 7:00 A.M. There is limited parking at the end of Indian School Road NE after 6:00 A.M. The parking area closes at 7:00 P.M. October to May and at 9:00 P.M. April to September.

FEES
None

SPECIAL CONSIDERATIONS AND HAZARDS
- Rattlesnakes: Rattlesnakes are a possibility during warm weather.
- Poison ivy: If you decide to hike up to the spring, it is best to wear long pants, as poison ivy often grows along sources of water.
- Harvester ants: These pesky anthills abound.

FACILITIES
- Accessibility: The trails are uneven and have a loose granite surface. People with limited mobility can safely bird around the perimeters of the parking lots or along Haines Avenue NE.
- Restrooms: None available. The closest restroom is in the mini-mart at Tramway and Menaul Boulevards NE.
- Water: None available
- Picnic tables: There is a picnic shelter along Trail #401 north of the Indian School Road NE parking area.

FOOD, GAS, AND LODGING
There are numerous restaurants and gas stations throughout Albuquerque. Lodging is concentrated at most exits along I-25 and I-40.

DESCRIPTION

The Open Space and trails at the east end of Copper Avenue NE are at the southern end of the foothills at an elevation of 5,900 feet. This location is another of the areas with access to good birding. It is the most easily reached foothills Open Space from public transportation. Many backyards in the residential area adjacent to the Open Space have feeders that attract a variety of birds.

The area is dominated by a large cone-shaped hill, covered with copper-colored boulders, called the U-Mound. The letter *U* once was painted on the side of the hill during an old college rivalry. Vestiges of white paint can be seen on a few of the boulders.

Enter the Open Space on the main trail (#400), which leads straight ahead until you reach Trail #401. Turn left onto the trail, and scan the large stand of cholla cactus on your left for Cactus Wren and Curve-billed Thrasher. Just before you come to an arroyo, check out the large juniper, which may be productive for Bushtit or Juniper Titmouse.

Retrace your steps to Trail #400, and turn left until it intersects Trail #365. Turn left onto the trail, and follow #365 along the south side of U-Mound; then continue up the narrow, switchback trail. The trail leads through a "pass" behind the mound. There are wooden barriers (that can serve as handrails) placed at strategic points to allow vegetation regrowth. Because of the rugged nature of part of this trail, many hikers prefer to use a walking stick to prevent falls on the disintegrating granite. The trail at this point runs under the power lines and is primarily used by runners and mountain bikers. It may be worthwhile checking out the habitat along this trail for a short portion. Return by retracing your steps.

As you return to the trailhead, you might want to consider walking along Trail #375 (turn left off Trail #400) for a short distance if you have not yet been successful in spotting a Cactus Wren. It has also nested in the cholla along this trail.

County: Bernalillo

eBird Hotspot: No

TARGET BIRDS

Scaled Quail The male is most easily seen during the breeding period, calling from a rock as it patrols its territory. It has also been seen sitting on the wall

U-Mound

behind the residential area. During other times of year, if you are lucky, you might see one or more scurry out from under the scrub and cross the trail.

Ash-throated Flycatcher It is a summer breeder and can be anywhere in the flat areas of the open space.

Pinyon Jay Itinerant roving flocks come down from the mountains at the end of January. By the late spring, there are only a few and are more intermittent. Neighborhood residents have reported them at their feeders, so be sure to check any feeders at houses adjacent to the Open Space. Please respect the privacy of the homeowners.

Curve-billed and Crissal Thrashers These are both year-round residents. The Curve-billed is a "can't miss" bird and can be seen in cholla cactus in this area. The Crissal Thrasher is a "maybe" bird.

Cactus Wren It is a year-round resident and breeder and has been seen in the cholla adjacent to the residential area and south of the main trail (#400) that leads to Trail #365. The best time to see one is in the late winter when it is establishing its territory and is most vocal, on through the breeding period. It is also more visible in early fall when building its roost nest.

Canyon Towhee It will be easy to see perched on bushes or signs, as well as flitting in the underbrush.

Black-throated, Black-chinned, and Rufous-crowned Sparrows The Rufous-crowned Sparrow is a year-round resident and breeder, while the Black-chinned and Black-throated Sparrows are summer breeders, arriving toward the end of March. All three forage on the ground and remain hidden in the scrub outside breeding season; however, they respond to pishing. The Black-throated is the most common and most easily seen. During breeding season, it often

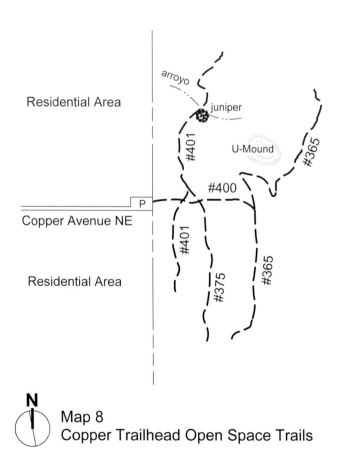

Map 8
Copper Trailhead Open Space Trails

Scaled Quail

can be found singing on top of four-wing saltbushes or cholla. After a brief song, it retreats to the bushes. Look for the Rufous-crowned near the base of U-Mound, often sitting briefly on boulders, making it difficult to spot. Scott's Oriole It is a summer resident, arriving mid-April and generally leaving by the end of August. It prefers to nest behind the mound. The male may be seen when it is out on a scouting mission.

OTHER BIRDS

Ladder-backed Woodpecker often can be seen in the cholla. Say's Phoebe can easily be seen here year-round. Western Scrub-Jay and Spotted Towhee, also year-round permanent residents and breeders, can be seen in the area behind U-Mound. Look for Rock Wren in the boulders, and listen for the Canyon Wrens around the back of the mound. House Finch is very prevalent in this area of the foothills at all times of the year. It particularly likes to feed on the seed heads of the Apache plume during its long blooming season. You may be lucky and see a Greater Roadrunner.

May migrants include Green-tailed Towhee; Chipping Sparrow; and McGillivray's, Virginia's, Wilson's, and Yellow-rumped Warblers.

Western Bluebird and Townsend's Solitaire are seen during the winter months. You will find an occasional Northern Flicker and flocks of Bushtits, White-crowned Sparrows, and Dark-eyed Juncos in the bushes. Because the foothills level off south of this location, it is a good place to look for raptors during the winter or when they are migrating north over the mountains. In addition to Cooper's and Red-tailed Hawks, you might see a Merlin or Peregrine Falcon. Raptors like to perch on the ridge south of the mound.

Western and Cassin's Kingbirds and Black-chinned Hummingbirds are summer breeders.

DIRECTIONS

By car: From the intersection of I-25 and I-40 in Albuquerque, travel approximately 7.5 miles east on I-40 to Exit 167 and take Tramway Boulevard NE north 1 mile to Copper Avenue NE. Turn right (east). Drive 0.75 mile until the street ends at the trailhead parking area.

Public transportation: Albuquerque city bus 11 serves the area. Earliest weekday arrival is 6:45 A.M.; on weekends, 8:00 A.M. The nearest stop on route 11 is at the intersection of Turner Drive NE and Copper Avenue NE. The walk to the Copper Trailhead is approximately 0.3 mile.

PARKING

Parking at the trailhead is very limited; however, street parking is available on the north side of Copper Avenue NE along the flood-control arroyo.

FEES

None

SPECIAL CONSIDERATIONS AND HAZARDS

- Rattlesnakes: Keep your eyes and ears alert for rattlesnakes during warm weather.
- Harvester ants: They are found on or near the trails.

FACILITIES

- Accessibility: All trails are single track; many are uneven and have loose granite.

- Restrooms: None available. The closest restrooms are at the gas station mini-mart at Lomas Boulevard NE, the next signal north of Copper Avenue NE on Tramway Boulevard NE.
- Water: None available
- Picnic tables: None available

There are numerous restaurants and gas stations throughout Albuquerque. Lodging is concentrated at most exits along I-25 and I-40.

Three Gun Spring (Tres Pistolas) and HawkWatch Trails

DESCRIPTION

This foothills site is accessed through the community of Carnuel, off I-40 as it begins to head into Tijeras Pass on the southern end of the Sandia Mountains. The trailhead is at an elevation of 6,200 feet.

The search for birds in this area begins as you wind through the twists and turns in the residential neighborhood. Drive slowly, and without using binoculars, scan the plants around each house, which often harbor a variety of birds, including Curve-billed and Crissal Thrashers and Canyon Towhee year-round, as well as seasonal specialties. Be sure to respect the privacy of the residents as you do this, as some will not want visitors peering into their yards with binoculars.

Start your walk at the end of the small parking area on Three Gun Spring Trail #05194, where you will enter U.S. Forest Service land (Sandia Ranger District). Large boulders dot the landscape near the trail in the desert scrub habitat of chamisa (rabbit brush), gray oak, and one-seed juniper. The Forest Service land extends for about 0.5 mile to the boundary of the Sandia Mountain Wilderness Area. Just inside the wilderness area, the trail forks. The right fork proceeds up Trail #05215 to the HawkWatch site, and the left fork continues on Trail #05194.

The well-marked trail up to the HawkWatch site is very steep with loose, disintegrating granite. The footing is sometimes difficult on the descent. The trail climbs 1,200 feet in a little over a mile to the observation site, and another 500 feet to the trapping blind. During spring migration, trained volunteers from HawkWatch International usually count and band raptors every day from February 24 through May 5 each year. Due to financial constraints, HawkWatch may not be able to continue to support the spring count. It is advisable to call the Albuquerque HawkWatch office (505-255-7622) or Salt Lake City (800-726-4295 or 810-484-6808) if the Albuquerque office is closed. Of course, the hawks will fly whether there is anyone there from HawkWatch or not.

Up to 18 species of raptors have been identified, with totals averaging between 3,200 and 6,500 migrants counted along this section of the Rocky Mountain branch of the Central Flyway. If you choose not to make the trek up to the HawkWatch site at 7,400 feet, take time to scan the skies if you visit during this period of time. Before your trip, it is helpful to download one of the diagrams of flight silhouettes of the seven types of raptor profiles from the HawkWatch Web site (www.hawkwatch.org/news-and-events/330 hmana).

The Three Gun Spring Trail gradually gains altitude, and piñon pines and mountain mahogany become more prevalent. Behind you is a view of Tijeras Canyon and the Manzanita Mountains. A small arroyo meanders through the foothills on your right as you ascend the trail lined with gray oak and mountain mahogany, often alive with birds. The trail is worth following for about 0.75 mile before switchbacks begin in the north end of the canyon. This south-facing trail is particularly pleasant during the winter.

County: Bernalillo

eBird Hotspot: Tres Pistolas

TARGET BIRDS

Scaled Quail It is a year-round resident and breeder. Although both Scaled and Gambel's Quail can be found in this area, the Scaled Quail is much more common. Both species are easiest to locate during breeding season. At other times of the year you might happen upon them bustling between bushes in the residential neighborhood and along the beginning of the trail.

Cassin's Kingbird This species of kingbird is a summer resident and breeder, also arriving at the end of April. Look for it perched near the tops of larger trees.

Juniper Titmouse It is fairly easy to find once you reach the part of the trail where the piñon pines become more widespread. Listen for its raspy call, and then look within the branches of the pines or junipers.

Bewick's Wren This wren is a year-round resident and breeder. Look for its activity in medium-sized shrubs. During breeding season, it often can be heard singing from the tops of these bushes.

Entering wilderness area along Three Gun Spring Trail

Blue-gray Gnatcatcher It is a summer resident, arriving at the end of April. It can be seen busily foraging in piñon pine or juniper bushes. Listen for its whiny call to help you locate it.

Curve-billed and Crissal Thrashers These two species are year-round residents and breeders and are easily seen as you drive through the residential area, as well as along the trail, particularly in the Open Space.

Scott's Oriole This is a good location to find Scott's Oriole, since it prefers canyon habitat. Start looking for it as you drive through the residential area.

OTHER BIRDS

The most pervasive bird here is the Western Scrub-Jay. It announces its presence, except during the period when feeding its young, as it sails from one piñon pine or bush to another. Other year-round residents and breeders

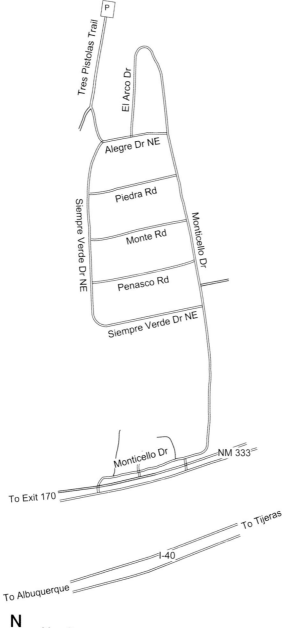

Tres Pistolas Trail

P

El Arco Dr

Alegre Dr NE

Piedra Rd

Siempre Verde Dr NE

Monte Rd

Monticello Dr

Penasco Rd

Siempre Verde Dr NE

Monticello Dr — NM 333

To Exit 170

To Tijeras

I-40

To Albuquerque

N

Map 9
Driving directions – Monticello Neighborhood
to Three Gun Spring Trailhead

include Mourning and White-winged Doves, Northern Flicker, Common Raven, Bushtit, Rock and Canyon Wrens, American Robin, Canyon and Spotted Towhees, and Lesser Goldfinch. You might happen upon a Greater Roadrunner either in the residential area or along the lower part of the trail.

During the spring raptor migration, you have a good chance of spotting Osprey, Northern Harrier, Sharp-shinned and Red-tailed Hawks, American Kestrel, or Golden Eagle. You might see Cooper's Hawk at any time of year.

During the winter, Townsend's Solitaire is often present, and White-crowned Sparrows are abundant in the residential neighborhood and along the trail. Dark-eyed (Gray-headed) Juncos migrate to lower elevations and can be seen easily.

During late spring and summer, Black-chinned and a few Broad-tailed Hummingbirds nest in the canyon. Chipping, Rufous-crowned, and Black-chinned Sparrows are summer residents but harder to see.

DIRECTIONS

By car: From the intersection of I-25 and I-40 in Albuquerque, drive east on I-40 approximately 9.5 miles to Exit 170, Carnuel. Travel east on NM 333 (Historic Route 66) for approximately 2 miles. At Monticello Drive (small street sign in the median and brown hiking sign by street), turn left and take an immediate right up the curve. After approximately 0.5 mile, turn left on Alegre Road NE. Continue 0.1 mile to Siempre Verde Drive NE. Bear right, traveling 0.2 mile on Tres Pistolas (dirt) to the trailhead.

Public transportation: None available

PARKING

The parking area is small and undeveloped. Signs are posted warning visitors not to leave valuables in their vehicles.

FEES

None

SPECIAL CONSIDERATIONS AND HAZARDS

- Rattlesnakes: Encountering a rattlesnake is always a possibility during warm weather.
- Harvester ants: Keep an eye out for this pesky ant on or near the trail.

- Accessibility: The parking lot is uneven. The trails are single track, often uneven with loose granite, and in some locations, extremely steep.
- Restrooms: None available. The closest restrooms are at commercial establishments at the intersection of Tramway Boulevard and East Central Avenue in Albuquerque.
- Water: None available
- Picnic tables: None available

FOOD, GAS, AND LODGING

Food, gas, and lodging are available approximately 3.5 miles west on NM 333 (Historic Route 66) to East Central Avenue and Tramway Boulevard in Albuquerque.

CHAPTER 5

Sandia Mountains

General Overview

The six sites in the Sandia Mountains area cover four distinct life zones, starting with the Ojito de San Antonio Open Space located in a piñon-juniper habitat, dominated by piñon-juniper woodlands on drier slopes and box elder, willow, and cottonwood in the montane riparian area. Sulphur Canyon and Doc Long and Cienega Picnic Areas are located in the life zone that has the highest plant diversity and is dominated by ponderosa pines. By the time you reach Capulin Spring Picnic Area, you will be in the mixed conifer zone. Sandia Crest, at 10,678 feet, is located in the spruce-fir zone. Each of these life zones attracts a different set of birds during both summer and winter. Birds that may breed at higher elevations often migrate to lower levels to spend the winter.

Expect a 20°F differential between the Cedar Crest area and Sandia Crest, and an even greater differential from the temperature in Albuquerque. During the summer months, the mornings may start out sunny and clear, but by noon big, puffy, white clouds can form, often followed quickly by a thunderstorm. Lightning is a concern.

While all of central New Mexico is at a higher altitude than much of the rest of the country, the effects of altitude are most noticeable in the mountains. See information on altitude in chapter 2.

General Directions

By car: For birding sites in the Sandia Mountains, begin at the intersection of I-25 and I-40 in Albuquerque. Drive east on I-40 approximately 14.5

miles to Exit 175, Tijeras (NM 337/NM 333). Immediately after the exit, the ramp divides. Take the left fork (Cedar Crest/NM 14 N), and merge onto Highway 66 E (NM 333; Historic Route 66). At the traffic light, continue north on NM 14 N (Turquoise Trail) for approximately 6 miles. The Ojito de San Antonio site is accessed from NM 14. At the intersection with NM-536 (Sandia Crest Road), turn left. The remaining sites in this section are accessed along the 13-mile road to the summit of the Sandia Mountains.

Public transportation: Available for Sandia Crest only via Sandia Peak Aerial Tramway (see Sandia Crest site description)

Ojito de San Antonio Open Space

DESCRIPTION

The Ojito de San Antonio Open Space, off NM 14 just north of I-40, is a secluded gem nestled behind the old church at San Antonio de Padua. The undeveloped 168-acre site is part of the Bernalillo County Open Space system. The trailhead is at an elevation of 6,600 feet.

As you approach the Open Space, you will be greeted by the sound of rushing water, which originates from springs on private property north of the Open Space. The water flows through a series of acequias (irrigation ditches) built in the mid-1800s to supply water to the original village of San Antonito de Padua. The Acequia Madre de San Antonio Community Ditch Association continues to care for the water and ditch system in conjunction with Bernalillo County. The water passes under the path to a fenced marshy area, normally unproductive for birds. However, the piñon-juniper habitat on either side of this section of the trail often can be very productive.

The trail, remnants of an old rutted road, wanders through a montane riparian area and vestiges of an apple orchard that often are alive with bird activity from spring through midsummer. During the summer, a variety of grasses and wildflowers grow along the road and between the apple trees. Because the area is more sheltered than the surrounding locality, it also provides good habitat for birds during the winter.

In the late spring and early summer, it can be productive to walk under the canopy created by the large willows and cottonwood trees. Although the dirt beneath the trees is normally bare, poison ivy grows on the edges, between the ruts in the road, and beside the acequia that crosses the road and runs under the trees.

Birder walking into Open Space during winter

A short distance beyond this stand of trees, the "road" ends and the trail continues into piñon-juniper habitat. As you ascend the incline, scan the utility wires, often a favorite perching spot for a variety of seasonal birds. At this point, there is a network of informal trails meandering along the ridge. A fence runs along the boundary of the Open Space.

Note: The Open Space is closed from August 15 to November 30 when bears roam through the orchard, gorging themselves on the apples.

County: Bernalillo

eBird Hotspot: Ojito de San Antonio Open Space

Ash-throated Flycatcher There are several pairs that spend the summer and breed in the riparian area. You can hear the calls as soon as you enter the meadow and should have no trouble spotting one.

Plumbeous and Warbling Vireos Both vireos are summer breeders. The best place to look for either one is in the trees near the large willows and cottonwoods.

Juniper Titmouse It is a year-round resident and breeder and can be found in the piñon-juniper habitat. Listen for its buzzy call.

Blue-gray Gnatcatcher It nests in the Open Space. Search for it in the piñon-juniper habitat.

Cedar Waxwing This is a good location for this species during the winter and migration. It often mingles within flocks of American Robins in the riparian area or on the neighboring farm, visible from the fence line. Do not enter private property.

Western Tanager It is a prevalent summer breeder and can be seen throughout the riparian area.

Black-headed Grosbeak It also is a common summer breeder in the riparian area.

OTHER BIRDS

Year-round residents include Downy and Hairy Woodpeckers, Northern Flicker, Western Scrub-Jay, Mountain Chickadee, Bushtit, White-breasted Nuthatch, Bewick's Wren, American Robin, and Spotted and Canyon Towhees. Although they do not nest or roost here, American Crows and Common Ravens can be seen here year-round, with crows being particularly common during the winter.

Summer residents include both Black-chinned and Broad-tailed Hummingbirds and Lesser Goldfinch. Black-throated Gray Warbler sometimes nests here.

Western Bluebird, Townsend's Solitaire, and Dark-eyed Junco are winter residents.

DIRECTIONS

By car: See General Overview in this chapter for directions to the traffic light, where you continue north on NM 14 N (Turquoise Trail). After 1 mile, turn left on a dirt road at the historic adobe San Antonio de Padua Church.

A small parking area for the Open Space trailhead is behind the church on the right.

Public transportation: None available

PARKING

A limited number of parking places are available adjacent to the trailhead.

FEES

None

SPECIAL CONSIDERATIONS AND HAZARDS

- Poison ivy: Poison ivy grows along the main path (often obscured by wild rose), beside the path leading to the large willow tree, and near the acequia that flows from under the willow.
- Bears: The Open Space is closed during the time of year when bears frequent the area, but they may also be present at other seasons.
- Rattlesnakes: Keep your eyes and ears alert for rattlesnakes during warm weather.

FACILITIES

- Accessibility: The remnants of the old road that form the first part of the trail often are rutted and can be extremely muddy during the winter. The other trails are unimproved.
- Restrooms: None available. The nearest restroom can be found at a mini-mart about 1 mile north of the Open Space on NM 14.
- Water: None available
- Picnic tables: They are planned for the future.

FOOD, GAS, AND LODGING

There are several restaurants and bed-and-breakfast establishments along NM 14, about 1–2 miles north in the community of Cedar Crest or 1 mile south in the Village of Tijeras along NM 333 (Historic Route 66). The nearest hotels are in Albuquerque at most exits along I-40 and I-25.

DESCRIPTION

The Sandia Crest Highway (NM 536), a National Scenic Byway, extends from Sandia Park on NM 14 up to Sandia Crest, the Sandia Mountains summit. It winds through four life zones along its 13.5 miles, starting at an elevation of 6,850 feet, reaching 10,678 feet at the Sandia Crest parking lot. There are a number of stops along the way that are worth a look for specific species of birds. Four of the stops are significant enough that a separate site description in this guide is devoted to them (Cienega Canyon, Sulphur Canyon and Doc Long Picnic Areas, Capulin Spring Picnic Area, and Sandia Crest). Others are summarized in this section.

For a more in-depth mile-by-mile description of this highway, please refer to www.rosyfinch.com/sandia.html#A_GUIDE_TO_THE_CREST_ROAD.

You will pass the turnoffs to Cienega Canyon and Sulphur Canyon and Doc Long Picnic Areas (described separately).

Tree Spring Trailhead: The trailhead will be on your left as you drive up the highway just past milepost 5 at an elevation of 8,609 feet. This spot is well known as a location to listen for owls after dark during the spring and summer.

Turnout 0.5 mile beyond Dry Camp Picnic Area: This turnout will be on your right as you head up the highway. The parking area often is muddy in places at this nondescript stop; however, it can be surprisingly productive for spotting birds. Check both the tops and the bases of the trees. Because of its proximity to the Sandia Peak Ski Area, this area may be crowded with parked vehicles during ski season.

Sandia Peak Ski Area lower parking lot: Drive into the lower parking lot on your right, just after passing the entrance to the ski area. Search the low shrubs and trees around the edge of the parking area. At the far edge, directly across from the entrance, is a good place to listen for the Northern Pygmy-Owl, which has been known to nest in the area below the parking lot. Study the power poles and wires over the parking lot. The owl historically has been known to sit there regularly but has not been seen in recent years. Check the aspens and elm trees across the road from the parking-lot entrance.

Balsam Glade Picnic Area: The picnic area is located on your right at the intersection with NM 165, at an elevation of 8,651 feet. There is a 0.3-mile

Trail to overlook at Balsam Glade

level nature trail that leads through stands of white fir, ponderosa pine, and Gambel oak to an overlook above Madera Canyon and NM 14 just northeast of Sandia Park. Raptors often can be seen circling in the thermals over the canyon, and Northern Goshawk nests in the canyon below the overlook. This area has been designated as an eBird Hotspot.

You will pass the turnoff to Capulin Spring Picnic Area (described separately).

Nine Mile Picnic Area: Yellow-rumped Warbler, Ruby-crowned and Golden-crowned Kinglets, and Dark-eyed Junco nest here. It is usually closed during the winter.

10K Trailhead: Located at 10,000 feet in elevation just past milepost 11, this trailhead is in the lower range of the spruce-fir habitat. There are two parking areas, one on either side of the road. The lower parking area is the trailhead for the northern portion of the 10K Trail. Below the parking area is a large open area that provides a good vantage point to spot birds that prefer the open meadow as well as birds that nest or perch in the tall trees beyond. Violet-green Swallows nest in the trunks of the ponderosa. The lower parking lot normally is filled with snowshoers and families sledding when there is an abundant snowpack.

The upper parking area is the trailhead for the southbound 10K Trail, which leads through the woods, and a cross-country ski trail that heads up and across the meadow and runs adjacent to the stand of young aspens, where Dusky Flycatcher may be found from June through August. As the trail winds into the trees, begin to look for American Three-toed Woodpecker.

Ellis Trailhead: At 10,260 feet, the Ellis Trailhead parking lot will be on the left and may not be visible until you pass it. The Ellis Trail leads north (across the highway). Also walk the trail south past the locked Sandia Peak Aerial Tram service road gate. After approximately 0.25 mile, this trail intersects several spur trails leading to those mentioned in the Sandia Crest site description where the American Three-toed Woodpecker has been seen.

County: Bernalillo

TARGET BIRDS

Northern Goshawk Even though it is a resident breeder, this accipiter is scarce and not always seen. It nests below the Balsam Glade Nature Trail overlook. There is a visual display at the Balsam Glade overlook that shows how its flight profile differs from that of other accipiters.

Band-tailed Pigeon Watch for one during the summer months perched in the very tops of trees along the Crest Highway, including at the turnout 0.5 mile beyond Dry Camp, the 10K Trailhead, and the service road south of Ellis Trailhead.

Northern Saw-whet Owl It is a nomadic, year-round breeder that does not return to the same nesting site each year. The best time to attempt to see one is during the nesting period, March through May. It has been heard and has nested in old woodpecker nest cavities, starting at milepost 3. You should have the most success hearing one at dusk, March through early June, at the Tree Spring Trailhead and Capulin Spring Picnic Area near the entrance to the Snow Play Area.

Northern Pygmy-Owl This owl is a scarce resident breeder, primarily in ponderosa and mixed conifer habitats. Since it is diurnal, it can be seen perched in the open during daylight hours. In the past, it has nested in the trees below the Sandia Peak Ski Area lower parking lot and has been seen from time to time perched on the power lines across the parking area. In the winter, it has been seen at Sandia Crest.

Red-naped Sapsucker It is a summer resident. A good place to find one is in the trees bordering the lower parking lot of the Sandia Peak Ski Area, the trees across from this parking lot, or the service road at Ellis Trailhead.

Cordilleran Flycatcher It is a summer breeder. Look for it at the group picnic shelter in July at Balsam Glade, where it often nests. You can also hear its distinctive song as you walk along the Balsam Glade Nature Trail.

Violet-green Swallow It can be seen flying over the meadows on either side of the 10K or Ellis Trail parking areas.

Grace's Warbler It is a summer breeder and often can be heard singing from the tops of the ponderosa pines at the Tree Spring Trailhead.

Red Crossbill It is a year-round resident. Look for it perched on the tops of conifers, starting at the turnout 0.5 mile beyond Dry Camp. The 10K Trailhead is a particularly good location.

OTHER BIRDS

Northern Flicker, Hairy Woodpecker, and Dark-eyed Junco are easily visible from the parking areas for the described sites year-round. If you wander into the woods, you can see or hear Mountain Chickadee; Pygmy, White-breasted, and Red-breasted Nuthatches; and Golden-crowned and Ruby-crowned Kinglets. American Three-toed Woodpecker has been seen on the trails from the 10K parking area and near the Ellis Trailhead. Other year-round birds include American Robin and Spotted Towhee.

During the spring and summer, you may hear Hermit Thrush calling from the woods as you drive along. Green-tailed Towhee might be seen at any of these spots. Western Bluebird often is seen at the 10K Trailhead parking areas, and Dusky Flycatcher, in the forested areas adjacent to the cross-country ski trail on the south side of the 10K Trailhead. Grace's, Virginia's, and Yellow-rumped Warblers are possible at the 10K Trailhead and Balsam Glade.

During the winter, look for finches. Cassin's Finch can be found all along the Crest Highway. Occasionally Pine Grosbeak may be spotted from the 10K Trailhead up to Sandia Crest.

By car: From the intersection of NM 14 and NM 536 (see General Overview for directions to intersection), travel up the Sandia Crest National Scenic Byway (NM 536). The stops mentioned in this section are described in the order they are encountered on this 13.5-mile road to the summit. This road may be temporarily closed or very icy in winter when tire chains may be required.

Public transportation: None available

Each of the sites mentioned has designated parking, with the exception of the turnout 0.5 mile beyond Dry Camp; however, the turnout is large enough for someone to park and get out safely.

A day-use fee ($3.00) or access pass is required at all locations except the ski area lower parking lot and the turnout.

Bears are spotted near one of the trails from time to time. If you have a picnic at Balsam Glade (or elsewhere), do not leave food unattended, even for a short period of time, while you wander off to bird. Refer to safety guidelines in chapter 2.

- Accessibility: There is wheelchair-accessible parking at Balsam Glade, 10K, and Ellis Trailheads. Balsam Glade has a wheelchair-accessible restroom, and the Nature Trail is compacted gravel. The 10K Trail is single track and uneven. The Ellis Trail south follows the service road that leads to the aerial tram.
- Restrooms: Located at Balsam Glade, Nine Mile, 10K, and Ellis Trailheads
- Water: None available
- Picnic tables: Available at Balsam Glade

The Sandia Crest House Gift Shop and Restaurant is located at the end of NM 536, approximately 5 miles above Capulin Spring at the summit. More restaurants are near the intersection of NM 14 and NM 536. There are bed-and-breakfast establishments along NM 14 between Tijeras and the start of NM 536. Hotels are available in Albuquerque at most exits along I-40 and I-25.

Sulphur Canyon and Doc Long Picnic Areas

DESCRIPTION

These two picnic areas, at an elevation of 7,200 feet, are adjacent to each other just a short distance apart as you ascend the Crest Road (NM 536). The 0.2-mile Doc Long–Sulphur Connecting Trail (FST #345, also known as Wolf Creek Trail) links the two picnic areas. Sulphur Canyon is open May 1–September 15, dawn to dusk. Doc Long Picnic Area, adjacent to the highway, is open year-round, while the upper picnic area is open May 1–October 31, also dawn to dusk. (Note that the entrance to Sulphur Canyon is shared with the road that eventually leads to Cienega Canyon, a site described in this guide.) The predominant vegetation is ponderosa pine and Gambel oak. There is a montane riparian area in Sulphur Canyon on your right just past the entrance where the spring originates, and a small meadow near the entrance of Doc Long.

At Sulphur Canyon, scan the trees near the entrance and just beyond the fee station, particularly during migration. In the early morning during spring and summer, there is often a buzz of activity over and in the riparian area. Sulphur Canyon is not as popular as Doc Long with picnickers, including weekends, making it easier for birding.

Next, walk through the picnic area on the paved path until it joins the road. At this point, you can continue past the tables on the trail connecting the two picnic areas or return to your car on the road.

Doc Long is a popular spot for families on the weekends. The reserved shelters often have large gatherings. Stop briefly near these shelters in early summer to check for possible nesting Cordilleran Flycatchers. Then drive farther into the picnic area, and park near the end of the pavement. The gate to the upper picnic area is closed in winter, but you can still enter this area on foot. You might want to walk up the asphalt path about 100 yards until you reach the trailhead for the Bill Spring Trail. Then double back, and

Birders along Wolf Creek Trail at Doc Long Picnic Area

bird along the Doc Long–Sulphur Connecting Trail (Wolf Creek Trail), which can be especially productive during the fall.

County: Bernalillo

eBird Hotspots: Doc Long Picnic Area and Bill Spring Trail

TARGET BIRDS

Western Screech-Owl It has nested in Doc Long Picnic Area, sometimes perching during the daylight hours on a limb next to its nesting cavity.

Broad-tailed Hummingbird It arrives in mid-April and can be seen sitting on territory protecting its nesting and feeding areas or buzzing in and out of the trees near the entrances of both picnic areas. It also can be spotted over the riparian area at Sulphur Canyon, where the male often performs its dive displays in the early morning.

Red-naped Sapsucker A summer resident, it nests in Doc Long Picnic area.

Cordilleran Flycatcher It is a summer breeder, arriving early to mid-May, and is present through mid-September. A pair often nests under the roof of one of the reservation picnic shelters at Doc Long, where one of the pair stands guard on a support beam.

Plumbeous and Warbling Vireos Both are summer breeders. Watch for them as you walk along the paths and road.

Steller's Jay This jay is a year-round resident and can be heard and seen in the ponderosas at both locations.

Pygmy Nuthatch It is a year-round resident and breeder. It is often found in mixed flocks of other nuthatches and chickadees.

Grace's Warbler It is a summer resident and breeder found high up in the ponderosa pines between May and the end of August.

Virginia's Warbler It is a summer resident and breeder, arriving in mid-April, and is gone by the end of September. Search for it in the understory.

OTHER BIRDS

White-breasted and Red-breasted Nuthatches travel in mixed flocks with Mountain Chickadees year-round at both areas. Juniper Titmouse also can be seen here. Listen for the "tin-horn" call of the Red-breasted Nuthatch to signal the presence of a mixed flock. Its call sounds much farther away than

Broad-tailed Hummingbird (Photo by Bonnie L. Long)

it is in reality. Other year-round possibilities include Cooper's Hawk, Hairy Woodpecker, Brown Creeper, American Robin, Spotted Towhee, and Pine Siskin.

During the summer, you might find Western Tanager or Black-headed Grosbeak.

These areas are on the southward migration route for a number of warblers, including MacGillivray's, Townsend's, Wilson's, and Black-throated Gray. From time to time, eastern strays have been sighted. Williamson's Sapsucker has also been reported in Doc Long and Sulphur Canyon Picnic Areas during fall migration (September through early November).

DIRECTIONS

By car: From the intersection of NM 14 and NM 536 (see General Overview for directions to intersection), travel up the Sandia Crest National Scenic Byway (NM 536). At 1.8 miles, turn left into the area marked Cienega and Sulphur Canyon Picnic Areas. Doc Long Picnic Area is 0.2 mile beyond Sulphur Canyon. The Sandia Crest highway may be icy or closed after severe winter storms.

Public transportation: None available

PARKING

Parking is available in several locations in both picnic areas, including several wheelchair-accessible spots.

FEES

A day-use fee ($3.00) or access pass is required.

SPECIAL CONSIDERATIONS AND HAZARDS

- Bears: Sulphur Canyon is a key bear habitat and is closed annually to public entry from September 15 to October 31 and sometimes during early summer. At other times, be prepared for bears wandering through the picnic areas. Do not leave any food on a picnic table, even for a short period of time while you walk away to bird. Food and coolers may be confiscated by the U.S. Forest Service if left unattended. Refer to safety guidelines in chapter 2.
- Poison ivy: It grows in several locations along the paved trail and

under the oaks at Sulphur Canyon Picnic Area and along sections of the Doc Long–Sulphur Connecting Trail.
- Cougars: There have been cougar sightings in this area. Refer to safety guidelines in chapter 2.

FACILITIES
- Accessibility: There is a paved trail through Sulphur Canyon Picnic Area.
- Restrooms: A wheelchair-accessible restroom is available at Doc Long but not at Sulphur Canyon.
- Water: None available
- Picnic tables: Available in both areas

FOOD, GAS, AND LODGING
There is a restaurant just south of the intersection of NM 14 and NM 536 and several more approximately 2.5 miles south on NM 14 in the town of Cedar Crest. Gas is available at the intersection of NM 14 and NM 536. Bed-and-breakfast-style lodging is available just north of the intersection of NM 14 and NM 536. Several more bed and breakfasts are located 1 mile south toward Cedar Crest off Snowline Road. The nearest hotels are in Albuquerque at most exits along I-40 and I-25.

Cienega Canyon Picnic Area

DESCRIPTION
Although this spot is adjacent to Sulphur Canyon Picnic Area, the large, open, formerly wet meadow (cienega) toward the end of the road provides an additional type of habitat. Keep to your left at the entrance to the Sulphur Canyon Picnic Area, and drive about 0.5 mile. Turn right at the T intersection, and drive to the end of the pavement to the parking lot for the upper picnic area and Cienega Canyon Trailhead.

Begin your exploration by walking downhill along the pavement a short distance, turning left at the road heading to the group reservation area. Check out the trees and shrubs on either side of this section of road. Even though there will be a barrier across the road, you can walk around to the start of the paved (and Braille-signed) Nature Trail. Survey the willows along the creek as you make your way to the Nature Trail, particularly during spring and fall migrations. Before you begin walking on the

Entrance to Nature Trail

Nature Trail, inspect the ponderosas in the group reservation area. You have your choice of two routes for the Nature Trail. The right-hand branch is very flat and leads along the stream level with the willows. The left-hand fork continues slightly uphill through a pine-oak habitat before it shortly rejoins the other trail at the beginning of the meadow. Where the two forks converge, follow the Nature Trail beside the meadow until it ends at the road.

Walk back to the parking area on the right side of the road, scanning the bushes between the road and another small stream that runs alongside it.

After returning to the upper parking area, examine the stream and willows along the left side. The upper picnic area usually is not very productive for birding.

During the summer, stop at the lower picnic area's host site. The host, who has been at this location for many years, usually maintains hummingbird feeders (they may not be up if bear activity is prevalent). In addition to the two nesting hummingbirds, the feeders attract species that migrate south through the Sandia Mountains beginning in mid-July.

The road into the picnic area is closed during winter months (from November 1 to May 1). It is possible to explore the area during the winter; however, you must walk in. (It is about a mile to the Nature Trail from the gate.)

County: Bernalillo

eBird Hotspot: Cienega Canyon Trail

TARGET BIRDS

Flammulated Owl This tiny owl has nested here and is heard almost every summer. It is present from mid-May through August.

Cordilleran Flycatcher It is a summer resident and breeder, arriving early to mid-May and staying through mid-September. Listen for its distinctive vocalizations.

Plumbeous Vireo This vireo is a summer resident and breeder. It builds its nest in evergreens about 5 feet from the ground.

Juniper Titmouse It can be seen from mid-March through the end of October. It is most easily spotted in the group reservation area.

Townsend's Solitaire Primarily a fall and winter resident, it arrives mid-October and stays through mid-March.

Grace's Warbler It breeds high up in the ponderosa pines and is present between May and the end of August.

Virginia's Warbler It is a summer resident. Search for it in the understory. It arrives in mid-April and is gone by the end of September.

Western Tanager It is a summer resident that can be seen from early May through mid- to late September. It also can be encountered high in the ponderosas along the left side of the road, just before entering the upper parking area.

OTHER BIRDS

American Robin is present year-round and is the most plentiful bird in the picnic area at the end of the road. Other year-round birds and breeders include Cooper's Hawk; Steller's Jay; Pygmy, White-breasted, and Red-breasted

Nuthatches; Brown Creeper; and Mountain Chickadee. These birds are most often seen in the ponderosas in the group reservation area.

Other summer residents and breeders include Black-chinned and Broad-tailed Hummingbirds, Warbling Vireo, and Black-headed Grosbeak. Lesser Goldfinch and Pine Siskin buzz in and out of the sunflowers in the meadow starting mid-August.

Some of the site's main draws are the migrants that stop over beginning in late August as they wing their way south. Regular migrants include Orange-crowned, Townsend's, Yellow-rumped , Wilson's, and MacGillivray's Warblers. Find them in the middle story, often in the shrubs near the parking lot, as well as in the willows along the streams that run on either side of the meadow. In addition to warblers, during migration look for Olive-sided Flycatcher and Western Wood-Pewee. Both Rufous and Calliope Hummingbirds frequently visit the host's feeders from mid-July through September.

DIRECTIONS

By car: From the intersection of NM 14 and NM 536 (see General Overview for directions to intersection), travel up the Sandia Crest National Scenic Byway (NM 536). At 1.8 miles, turn left into the area marked Cienega and Sulphur Canyon Picnic Areas. Bear left to Cienega as described in the first paragraph of the Cienega Canyon Picnic Area site description.

Public transportation: None available

PARKING

Numerous parking areas, including wheelchair-accessible spots, are available throughout the picnic area.

FEES

A day-use fee ($3.00) or access pass is required.

SPECIAL CONSIDERATIONS AND HAZARDS

■ Bears: From time to time bears wander through the picnic areas, particularly in the early summer. Do not leave any food on a picnic table, even for a short period of time while you walk away to bird. Food and coolers left unattended may be confiscated by U.S. Forest Service patrols. Refer to safety guidelines in chapter 2.

- Cougars: There have been cougar sightings in this area. Refer to safety guidelines in chapter 2.
- Dead trees: Due to years of drought, disease, and insect infestation, thousands of trees have died in recent years. Until the U.S. Forest Service is able to clear all of the dead trees, there is a risk of death or serious injury from falling trees, especially during windy conditions.

FACILITIES

- Accessibility: The Nature Trail is paved and has Braille signs. The restroom across from the entrance-exit of the Nature Trail is wheelchair accessible.
- Restrooms: There are restrooms near the picnic areas and across from the Nature Trail.
- Water: None available
- Picnic tables: Picnic tables are scattered throughout the Cienega Canyon Picnic Area.

FOOD, GAS, AND LODGING

There is a restaurant just south of the intersection of NM 14 and NM 536 and several more approximately 2.5 miles south on NM 14 at the town of Cedar Crest. Gas is available at the intersection of NM 14 and NM 536. Bed-and-breakfast-style lodging is available just north of the intersection of NM 14 and NM 536. Several more bed and breakfasts are located 1 mile south toward Cedar Crest off Snowline Road. The nearest hotels are in Albuquerque at most exits along I-40 and I-25.

Capulin Spring Picnic Area

DESCRIPTION

The major attraction of this site, located in a mixed conifer habitat at an elevation of 8,840 feet, is "The Log," a hollowed-out horizontal log that collects dripping water from Capulin Spring. The actual spring is located within a fenced portion of the Capulin Spring Picnic Area adjacent to the log. During times of day when the log is in the shade, the water that pools in the bottom of the log attracts a variety of birds from spring through fall.

To reach the log viewing area, turn right as you enter the picnic area and drive a short way until you come to a barrier across the road. There is an

"The Log"

area to the right where you can park. The former picnic spot (first picnic table on your left) about 0.25 mile down the road provides a place to view the log. You can bring a lawn chair or sit on the ground, staying far enough away to allow the birds to come in freely. In addition to being alert for birds that fly into the shrubs behind the log and then drop down inside to drink or bathe, continually scan the nearby trees and the tops of the conifers a short distance back from the log. While most birds will eventually come into the log, many will only fly into the nearby trees.

You might also want to take a walk down the road that leads straight ahead from the entrance to the picnic area. During the summer, you can go into the adjacent Capulin Snow Play Area to look for Dusky Flycatcher that often nests in the periphery. Be alert near the Snow Play slopes as mountain bikers often careen down the steps and into the parking lot. Although the gate is open during the winter, it is difficult to bird when Snow Play Area users are present.

Capulin Spring Picnic Area is also a well-known site to listen for owls as dusk approaches and after dark. For the best opportunity to see or hear owls, drive straight into the picnic area and park in the spots adjacent to the barrier that leads to the Snow Play Area.

County: Bernalillo

eBird Hotspot: Capulin Spring

TARGET BIRDS

Band-tailed Pigeon This pigeon often flies into the trees near the log; the sound of its wings can signal that one or more has flown in and is perched nearby.

Flammulated Owl The parking lot just before the entrance to the Snow Play Area is a good place to hear, and perhaps see, this species from dusk into the evening, mid-May through August.

Northern Saw-whet Owl This owl can be heard calling in the same area as the Flammulated Owl, from March through early June.

Dusky Flycatcher Capulin Spring is one of the areas where this high-altitude summer resident and breeder can easily be seen. It is most easily seen by walking the perimeter of the Snow Play parking lot.

Yellow-rumped Warbler This is a very prevalent species at the log.

Green-tailed Towhee This striking towhee often visits the log.

Dark-eyed Junco It is the most common species that visits the log.

OTHER BIRDS

Year-round residents include Red-naped Sapsucker, Steller's Jay, Mountain Chickadee, White-breasted and Red-breasted Nuthatches, Brown Creeper, Ruby-crowned and Golden-crowned Kinglets, and Pine Siskin.

Summer residents may include Cordilleran Flycatcher, Hermit Thrush, Virginia's and Grace's Warblers (at the log), Western Tanager, and Black-headed Grosbeak.

During fall migration, look for Wilson's, MacGillivray's, Orange-crowned, and Townsend's Warblers as they come to drink at the log.

Winter residents include Clark's Nutcracker, Townsend's Solitaire, Cassin's Finch, and Red Crossbill. They can be seen in the main part of the picnic area.

By car: From the intersection of NM 14 and NM 536 (see General Overview for directions to intersection), travel up the Sandia Crest National Scenic Byway (NM 536) for approximately 8 miles. Capulin Spring Picnic and Snow Play Areas will be on the right.

Public transportation: None available

PARKING

A small parking area is available adjacent to the gated area that leads to the log. Parking for the other areas is available a short distance from the entrance.

FEES

A $3.00 U.S. Forest Service amenities fee or access pass is required.

SPECIAL CONSIDERATIONS AND HAZARDS

- Bears: Bears may be encountered anywhere in the Sandia Mountains. Refer to safety guidelines in chapter 2.
- Dead trees: A great number of trees have died recently from a bark beetle infestation. While the U.S. Forest Service has been actively involved removing trees that might pose a danger to the picnic area, visitors are warned to be alert for leaning dead trees that might topple over during high winds.

FACILITIES

- Accessibility: The road leading to the log often has debris on it with an incline that would not be suitable for wheelchairs.
- Restrooms: There are several restrooms scattered throughout the Picnic Area.
- Water: None available
- Picnic tables: There are picnic tables near the entrance to the Picnic Area.

FOOD, GAS, AND LODGING

The Sandia Crest House Gift Shop and Restaurant is located at the end of NM 536, approximately 5 miles above Capulin Spring at the summit. More restaurants are situated at the start of Sandia Crest Highway near the intersection of NM 14 and NM 536. Gas is available at the intersection of NM 14 and NM 536. Bed-and-breakfast-style lodging is available just north of the intersection of NM 14 and NM 536. Several more bed and breakfasts are located 1 mile south toward Cedar Crest off Snowline Road. The nearest hotels are in Albuquerque, where they are concentrated at most exits along I-25 and I-40.

Sandia Crest

DESCRIPTION

Located at the end of NM 536 at an elevation of 10,678 feet, the Crest House is known widely as the most easily reached location to observe all three species of rosy-finches during the winter. The Sandia Crest area (Sandia Mountains summit) is a prime birding location at all times of the year.

Investigate some of the outside areas before visiting the Sandia Crest House to watch the rosy-finches from early November through late March and the hummingbird feeders from mid-April through mid-October, if weather, trail, and road conditions permit. The Crest House is open from 9:30 A.M. to sunset (closed Thanksgiving and Christmas). Bad weather or

Rosy-finches on deck at Sandia Crest House

road conditions may result in additional closures, so call the Crest House if you are uncertain (505-243-0605).

Walk along the Crest Nature Trail, which starts just beyond the rest-rooms at the far end of the lower parking lot. The first part of the trail, for approximately 100 yards, is paved and accessible for wheelchairs or individuals with limited mobility. Just beyond is the beginning of a short trail (single track and often uneven) that travels along the ridgeline and then loops back (partially on stairs) through the trees of the spruce-fir habitat: quaking aspen, Engelmann spruce, corkbark fir, Douglas-fir, and limber and ponderosa pine. Signs identify each tree. Make particular note of the bark of the Engelmann spruce to assist you in locating the American Three-toed Woodpecker.

After returning to the parking lot, walk down the exit driveway and then turn to your right and walk along a rutted gravel road (Kiwanis Meadow Road) that leads to a stone structure built on a ridge promontory, known as Kiwanis Cabin (not visible from Kiwanis Meadow Road), checking for birds on either side of the road. Pass the entrance to the Crest Trail, #130. When you reach Kiwanis Meadow (bordered by wood rail fences), scout for birds that prefer the meadow habitat and its proliferation of wildflowers, particularly during the summer months. Stay on the trail to protect the fragile habitat. Continue on to the Kiwanis Cabin, where the trail ends, and its view of birds that utilize the thermals just below the overlook.

If you are looking for the American Three-toed Woodpecker and have not yet seen it, retrace your route and turn right on the Crest Trail. This trail is extremely rutted and has large roots that can be treacherous if you do not look down frequently as you walk. Continue along this trail to the sign "To Ellis Trailhead." Take this trail, which leads to the Switchback Trail (a cross-country ski trail marked with blue diamonds on the trees, Trail #271), for about 0.25 mile, and then return to the Crest Trail. The Crest Trail beyond this location leads (about 1.25 miles) to the Upper Tram Terminal. Halfway back along the Crest Trail, you can explore along a trail that may not be labeled (Buried Cable Trail #272) on your right, again walking along for about 0.25 mile before returning to the Crest Trail.

When you return to the Kiwanis Meadow Road, you can either return to the parking lot by the same route or take the trail that switchbacks up the hill and leads to the Crest Nature Trail. Be sure to visit the Sandia Crest House if you have not already done so.

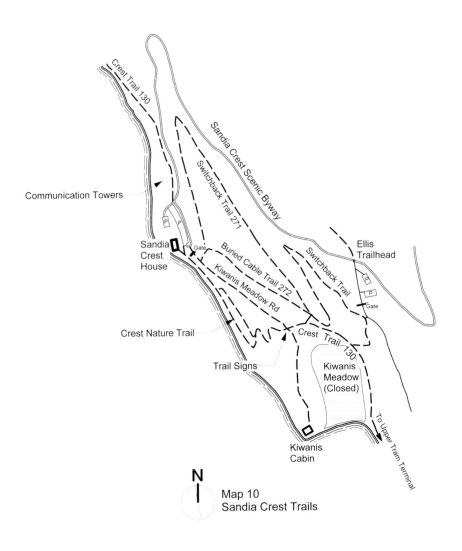

Communication Towers

Crest Trail 130

Sandia Crest Scenic Byway

Switchback Trail 271

Sandia Crest House

Gate

Buried Cable Trail 272

Kiwanis Meadow Rd

Switchback Trail

Ellis Trailhead

Gate

Crest Nature Trail

Trail Signs

Crest Trail 130

Kiwanis Meadow (Closed)

To Upper Tram Terminal

Kiwanis Cabin

N

Map 10
Sandia Crest Trails

County: Bernalillo
eBird Hotspot: Cibola NF—Sandia Crest

TARGET BIRDS

Calliope Hummingbird This tiny hummingbird migrates south through the Sandia Mountains and often can be seen from mid-July through September at the Crest House feeders.

American Three-toed Woodpecker This woodpecker has returned to the Sandia Crest area to take advantage of damage caused by bark beetle infestation and is a year-round resident and breeder. It nests in and flakes the bark off Engelmann spruce to scrounge for insects. It has been seen in the trees on the downhill side—about halfway down Kiwanis Meadow Road and on the other trails described in this section. Look for signs of fresh bark chips beneath the spruce. Although the American Three-toed Woodpecker might drill loudly to loosen the bark, it switches to flaking, which is a much more subtle sound than the hammer-pounding, drilling sound of the similar Hairy Woodpecker, which also inhabits these woods.

American Three-toed Woodpecker (Photo by Bonnie L. Long)

Clark's Nutcracker It is a year-round resident at high elevations in the Sandia Mountains; however, its itinerant behavior makes it difficult to see. The best opportunity is near the parking lot or along the ridge of the Crest Nature Trail in fall and winter or north along the Crest Trail adjacent to the communication towers.

Ruby-crowned and Golden-crowned Kinglets Ruby-crowned Kinglet nests high in the spruce and fir trees. Although these kinglets can be seen during the winter, many spend the winter at lower elevations. The Golden-crowned Kinglet is a year-round resident and also breeds high in the corkbark fir trees. Shortly after it has fledged, it sometimes can be seen near the ground, although it is best to know and recognize its call in order to locate it. Both species frequent the part of the Crest Nature Trail that loops through the woods or the informal trails.

Yellow-rumped Warbler It breeds at this location and can be seen in the trees along the road leading to Kiwanis Meadow.

Green-tailed Towhee It is a summer resident that prefers alpine meadow habitat. Look for it in Kiwanis Meadow.

Black, Brown-capped, and Gray-crowned Rosy-Finches, including the coastal (Hepburn's) subspecies The best location to observe these three species of rosy-finch in winter is from inside the Crest House. Purchase a hot drink and a snack, and then settle at one of the tables next to the window. The rosy-finches make an appearance every 15 to 20 minutes. Watch for a swirl of bird activity as the finches arrive in flocks. When they reach the apex of their whorl, they begin to drop and settle in the conifers about 50 feet from the feeder. One by one a few begin to venture to the trees just beyond where the feeder hangs at the corner of the deck. And then, as if someone has given a silent command, they mob the hanging platform feeder and devour seed on the snowy deck. As quickly as they arrive, they depart in a burst of energy. You can observe rosy-finch banding on Sundays, between at 9:30 A.M. and 1:30 P.M. from December through mid-March, weather permitting. If in doubt, call the Crest House.

Cassin's Finch This finch is an intermittent visitor to the Crest House feeders during the winter.

Red Crossbill It is a year-round resident and breeder at the Sandia Crest that is often observed near the parking lot perched on the very tops of conifers.

Year-round residents include Steller's Jay, which frequents the Crest House feeder during the winter at times when the finches are not present and sometimes can be spotted along one of the trails at other times of the year. Mountain Chickadee, Red-breasted and White-breasted Nuthatches, Brown Creeper, and Dark-eyed Junco are year-round residents and breeders that visit the feeders during the winter and inhabit the woods during the remainder of the year. Hairy Woodpecker, Northern Flicker, and American Robin also are year-round residents and breeders that can easily be seen along Kiwanis Meadow Road. Common Raven is present year-round although more plentiful during the winter.

Summer residents and breeders include Broad-tailed Hummingbird, House Wren, and Hermit Thrush. It is often possible to see either Violet-green Swallow or White-throated Swift circling in the thermals below the ridgeline on the Crest Nature Trail. Rufous Hummingbird migrates through starting in mid-July and can easily be seen at the Crest House feeders along with Broad-tailed Hummingbird.

DIRECTIONS

By car: From the intersection of NM 14 and NM 536 (see General Overview for directions to intersection), travel up the Sandia Crest National Scenic Byway (NM 536) 13.5 miles to its end at the summit. This road may be temporarily closed or very icy in winter.

Public Transportation (using Sandia Peak Aerial Tramway): At the top tram terminal, hikers may access the part of the Crest Trail (#130) leading to the Crest House. This 1.8-mile all-uphill trail (sometimes in deep snow) is not recommended in winter or for those not acclimated to hiking above 10,000 feet. From the intersection of I-25 and I-40 in Albuquerque, travel 8 miles east on I-40 to Exit 167, Tramway Boulevard NE (NM 556). Travel north on Tramway Boulevard NE approximately 7 miles to the three-way stop sign at the intersection of Tramway Boulevard NE and Tramway Road NE. Turn right (east) and proceed to the end, stopping to pay a small grounds fee at the kiosk. Buy tram tickets inside Sandia Peak Tramway facility for the 15-minute ride to the Four Seasons Visitor Center and restaurant. The approximately 1.8-mile trail to Sandia Crest House begins north of the restaurant and follows the ridgeline.

PARKING

There is a parking lot level with the entrance of the Crest House and a lower parking lot on the Crest Nature Trail level.

FEES

There is a $3.00 U.S. Forest Service amenities fee, or you can use a federal annual pass. A small grounds parking fee and a more substantial tram ticket cost apply for those accessing the summit via Sandia Peak Aerial Tramway.

SPECIAL CONSIDERATIONS AND HAZARDS

- Ice: During the winter there are icy spots on the path from the upper parking lot to the Crest House.
- Altitude: The effects of altitude can be unexpected and unpleasant at 10,000 feet, particularly for the visitor who normally lives at much lower elevations. Refer to safety guidelines in chapter 2.

FACILITIES

- Accessibility: There is designated wheelchair-accessible parking in both lots. The facility is wheelchair accessible, with a lift from the right entrance located at the same level as the parking lot. The path up to the building is often slippery during the winter. The Crest Nature Trail is paved for a short distance.
- Restrooms: There are wheelchair-accessible restrooms adjacent to both parking lots.
- Water: Bottled water can be purchased in the Crest House.
- Picnic tables: None available

FOOD, GAS, AND LODGING

The Sandia Crest House Gift Shop and Restaurant is located at the end of NM 536, approximately 5 miles above Capulin Spring at the summit. If you do any birding from inside the Crest House, please patronize the business. Gas is available at the intersection of NM 14 and NM 536. Bed-and-breakfast-style lodging is available just north of the intersection of NM 14 and NM 536. Several more bed and breakfasts are located 1 mile south toward Cedar Crest off Snowline Road. The nearest hotels are in Albuquerque at most exits along I-40 and I-25.

CHAPTER 6

Manzanita and Manzano Mountains

General Overview

These six sites are in a variety of habitats on NM 337 and NM 55. NM 337 crosses first through the Manzanita Mountains, which form a bridge between the Sandia and the Manzano Mountains. Although the Manzano Mountains officially start about 25 miles south, the distinction is imperceptible to the visitor. The first few miles of the road wind through piñon-juniper woodlands, which in some locations transition to an oak-pine habitat. This section of NM 337 falls within Bernalillo County.

You will leave Bernalillo County and enter Torrance County. NM 337 ends at NM 55, which you will then follow for the rest of the route. (See specific directions below.) It traverses a largely piñon-juniper area, much of which has been cleared for farming and ranching. Fourth of July Canyon is in a pine-oak habitat, and the Capilla Peak area is in the mixed conifer zone.

Each vegetation type attracts a different set of birds during both summer and winter. Birds that may breed at higher elevations often migrate to lower levels to spend the winter.

As in the Sandia Mountains, there is a temperature differential between sites along NM 337 / NM 55 and sites at higher elevations. These mountainous areas are also subject to summer thunderstorms. The effects of altitude are especially apparent at Fourth of July Canyon and more particularly, Capilla Peak.

General Directions

Start from the intersection of I-25 and I-40 in Albuquerque, and travel east on I-40 approximately 14.5 miles to Exit 175, Tijeras (NM 337/NM 333). At the Village of Tijeras, drive south on NM 337. Check your fuel gauge, as gas stations are scarce until the town of Mountainair (54 miles). Refer to specific sites for directions from this point.

Along the Manzanita and Manzano Mountains

DESCRIPTION

NM 337 extends from I-40 at Tijeras to just before the village of Tajique, where it ends at a T intersection with NM 55, which then heads south to Mountainair, a distance of 54 miles. Most of the road passes through private property, including the historic Spanish Land Grant villages of Chilili, Torreon, Tajique, and Manzano. Please respect private property and any signs that post restrictions.

A number of locations along the way are worth a stop to take advantage of specific varieties of birds. Some sites are significant enough that a separate description is devoted to them. Others are summarized in this section.

NM 337 Highway Birding: Some of the best birding along NM 337 is from the roadside, where birds perch on power lines and fence posts or soar over the open grassland. The challenge is that in many areas, the shoulders of the highway slope away to facilitate water drainage, making it difficult to park. Be careful not to block anyone's private road or driveway in your quest to see a bird.

Pine Flat Picnic Area (Bernalillo County, 6.9 miles from I-40/NM 337) is located in a pine-oak habitat and offers the last public restroom for approximately 33 miles.

The junction where NM 217 meets NM 337 (Bernalillo County, 18 miles from I-40/NM 337) is a particularly good location for nesting Violet-green and Barn Swallows and has a spot on the right where you can pull off the highway.

Shortly after passing through the Spanish Land Grant town of Chilili (Bernalillo County, 22 miles from I-40/NM 337), you will notice a cemetery on your left. It is important to park outside the cemetery to search for sparrows. Lark Sparrow often is prevalent. Please be sensitive to the community's feelings toward outsiders.

Just past Chilili, you will leave Bernalillo County and enter Torrance County. Continue to drive south on NM 337 for another 5 miles to the intersection of NM 337 and NM 55. There is a large turnout just before the T intersection. Both at this location and immediately after you turn right and head west on NM 55, check for Mountain and Western Bluebirds, Horned Lark, American Kestrel, and Lazuli Bunting. Immediately after passing milepost 84, NM 55 makes a sharp left into the village of Tajique.

Shortly after entering Tajique (Torrance County), look for a creek that crosses the road. A paved road, Camino Lesperance, runs alongside it on the east. This is a worthwhile stop in the spring if there has been a wet winter and water is flowing in the creek. Yellow Warblers have been seen here during migration. Bullock's Orioles often nest in the large deciduous trees on the north side of the road. When you return to NM 55, immediately look for the brown sign on the right for Fourth of July Canyon (described separately).

Continue south on NM 55 for almost 9 miles, passing through the village of Torreon to the village of Manzano. As you enter the village, look for the church on your left. Forest Road 245 leading to Capilla Peak will be on your right, opposite the church (described separately).

Manzano Pond (Torrance County): Immediately beyond FR 245 is a small store, Manzano Tiendita. Turn right and drive a short distance to the parking area on your left. The small fishing lake is a wonderful place to spot birds from spring through fall migration. Before wandering around the perimeter of the pond, walk up the road about 0.25 mile, checking the hillside to the north as well as the marshy area along the creek that feeds into the pond. A variety of riparian birds can be seen here. Then walk inside the fence surrounding the pond, where you will be able to explore the margins. As you walk along the edge of the pond, be cognizant of the fact that Spotted Sandpipers nest on the ground near the water. Barn Swallows, and others during migration, swoop over the pond gleaning insects.

Just past the village of Manzano, look on your left for raised-earth stock ponds, often referred to as "tanks," which are good for Mallards and Blue-winged Teal, as well as occasional shorebirds and warblers during migration when there has been enough rain to allow the tanks to retain water. Scan the trees for possible Western Tanager and Bullock's Oriole.

The entrance to Salinas Pueblo Missions National Monument–Quarai Unit (described separately) is almost 9 miles south of Manzano.

Manzano Pond

Mountainair sewage ponds (Torrance County): Mountainair is approximately 17 miles south of County Road B076. At the intersection with U.S. 60, turn east for about 0.5 mile. The sewage ponds are just south of the highway. There is a dirt road just past the ponds that will lead you around to the back where you can view the ponds. A spotting scope will be an asset. A large variety of waterfowl spend either the winter or summer in these ponds. In addition, several species of shorebirds stop here during spring and fall migrations.

eBird Hotspots: Manzano Pond and Mountainair Sewage Ponds

American Kestrel You may encounter it perched on power lines or fences any-where along both NM 337 and NM 55.

Spotted Sandpiper It nests at Manzano Pond and can easily be found bobbing along the shore. It may stop over at the Mountainair sewage ponds during migration.

Pinyon Jay Watch for roving flocks, or during nesting season for single perched birds, between Chilili and the turnoff to Quarai.

Horned Lark It often is seen in the grassy area near the intersection of NM 337 and NM 55.

Violet-green and Barn Swallows Both swallows nest near the intersection of NM 337 and NM 217 and can be seen all along NM 55.

Western and Mountain Bluebirds Look for both of these species on wires along NM 337, NM 55, and the roads into Fourth of July Canyon and Quarai. Westerns are the most prevalent.

Lark Sparrow This sparrow can be seen between mid-April and the end of September at the Chilili cemetery, in the grassy areas near Manzano, and near the Mountainair sewage ponds.

OTHER BIRDS

Year-round species include Mallard, Mourning and Eurasian Collared-Doves, Northern Flicker, Say's Phoebe, Western Scrub-Jay, Common Raven, Mountain Chickadee, Juniper Titmouse, White-breasted Nuthatch, American Robin, Northern Mockingbird, European Starling, Dark-eyed (Gray-headed) Junco, Red-winged Blackbird, Western Meadowlark, and House Finch.

Species that are summer residents include Turkey Vulture, Common Nighthawk, Western Wood-Pewee, Western and Cassin's Kingbirds, Plumbeous and Warbling Vireos, Western Tanager, Vesper Sparrow, Black-headed Grosbeak, Bullock's Oriole, and Lesser Goldfinch.

Winter species include Northern Shoveler, Green-winged Teal, Ring-necked Duck and Lesser Scaup (Mountainair sewage ponds), Red-tailed Hawk, Song and White-crowned Sparrows, and American Goldfinch.

During migration look for Greater Yellowlegs, Western Sandpiper, Olive-sided Flycatcher, Northern Rough-winged Swallow, Yellow Warbler, and Chipping Sparrow.

By car: From the intersection of I-25 and I-40 in Albuquerque, travel east on I-40 approximately 14.5 miles to Exit 175, Tijeras (NM 337/NM 333). Drive south on NM 337 at Tijeras. The sites mentioned are located along 29 miles of NM 337 and then 24.7 miles of NM 55 to the town of Mountainair at U.S. 60.

Public transportation: None available

See individual place descriptions.

None

Parking may be difficult along the highway. Use caution and respect private property.

- Accessibility: None of these sites are wheelchair accessible.
- Restrooms: Available at Pine Flat Picnic Area and Manzano Pond
- Water: None available at specific sites. Bottled water can be purchased at the store in the village of Manzano.
- Picnic tables: Available at Pine Flat Picnic Area

Food is available in the Village of Tijeras near the intersection of NM 337 and I-40. Convenience-store-type food can be purchased at the Manzano Tiendita. Lodging and gas are available at the town of Mountainair near the intersection of NM 55 and U.S. 60. Other lodging is located at most exits along I-40 in the city of Albuquerque. Food, gas, and lodging are not readily available along the 54-mile distance of NM 377 and NM 55 between Tijeras and Mountainair.

Sandia Ranger District Visitor Center

DESCRIPTION

The Visitor Center for the Sandia Ranger Station in the Village of Tijeras is an excellent place to start a birding expedition in the Sandia or Manzanita/ Manzano Mountains. Located 0.5 mile south of the I-40/NM 337 interchange, at an elevation of 6,300 feet, the grounds have been managed for both wildlife habitat and fire control. It is located in a piñon-juniper habitat. The Visitor Center is open from 8:00 A.M. to 5:00 P.M. Monday through Friday and has a sightings clipboard, informational guides, and a small bookstore. Various types of annual passes are sold. Volunteers lead bird walks on Tuesday mornings, May through mid-October. Call 505-281-3304 to get information on starting times.

Begin your birding by scanning the perimeter of the parking area north of the Visitor Center. At all times of the year, birds can be found in the trees along the arroyo, north of the building, and on the wires.

Check the hillside across the highway for species perched in the trees, and then wander behind the Visitor Center. Birds often frequent the bushes in the arroyo on either side of the footbridge. Next, scan the trees on both sides of the trail just beyond the bridge. The trail meanders along another small arroyo and leads to the Tijeras Pueblo archeological site. Search the trees in the arroyo and the piñon pines and juniper along the trail.

County: Bernalillo

eBird Hotspot: No

TARGET BIRDS

Cassin's Kingbird It is a summer resident and breeds at this location. It frequently can be seen on the power lines adjacent to the parking lot.

Juniper Titmouse While it is not prevalent, it is a resident breeder. Look for it in the piñon pines near the archaeological site.

Western Bluebird It is a resident breeder, but the best time to spot one is from October through April, often on wires over the arroyo.

Chipping Sparrow It is a year-round resident and can be found in the arroyo and power lines adjacent to the parking lot.

OTHER BIRDS

Year-round birds include Northern Flicker, Western Scrub-Jay, Say's Phoebe, Bushtit, Bewick's Wren, American Robin, Canyon Towhee, House Finch, and

Trail to pueblo ruins

sometimes Mountain Chickadee. Red-tailed Hawk often soars above the hill behind the Tijeras Pueblo Interpretive Center.

Summer residents and breeders include Broad-tailed Hummingbird, Ash-throated Flycatcher, Black-headed Grosbeak, Bullock's Oriole, and Lesser Goldfinch.

Fall and winter residents include White-crowned Sparrow and Dark-eyed (Gray-headed) Junco.

During migration, look for Red-naped Sapsucker, Yellow-rumped Warbler, Western Tanager, and American Goldfinch.

DIRECTIONS

By car: From the intersection of I-25 and I-40 in Albuquerque, drive east on I-40 approximately 14.5 miles to Exit 175, Tijeras (NM 337/NM 333). Immediately after you exit I-40, the ramp divides. Take the right fork and

merge onto NM 337. At the traffic light, continue south on NM 337 for approximately 0.5 mile. The Sandia Ranger Station is on the left.
Public transportation: None available

There is a large lot with ample parking.

None

- Rattlesnakes: There is the possibility of rattlesnakes on the hillside near the Tijeras Pueblo site during the summer.
- Traffic: If the district is responding to a wildfire, there may be heavy traffic, including firefighting apparatus, entering and exiting the facility.

- Accessibility: It is possible for someone who uses a wheelchair to bird along the parking lot and onto the bridge over the arroyo. The trail beyond to the archaeological site is single track.
- Restrooms: A restroom is located next to the parking lot.
- Water: There is a drinking fountain near the restrooms.
- Picnic tables: None available

A couple of fast-food and pizza restaurants are located 0.5 mile north in the Village of Tijeras along NM 333 (Historic Route 66). The nearest gas station is about 1 mile north of Tijeras. Drive east on NM 333 from the intersection of NM 337 in Tijeras, and merge onto NM 14, heading north for 1 mile toward Cedar Crest. The nearest hotels are in Albuquerque off I-40.

Otero and Cedro Canyons
DESCRIPTION
This area in the Manzanita Mountains (the lower ridge between the Sandia and the Manzano mountain ranges) sustains both mature piñon-juniper and riparian habitats. It has been designated as an Important Bird Area by

the National Audubon Society and BirdLife International because it is a paramount nesting area for the Black-throated Gray Warbler and Gray Flycatcher.

The Otero Canyon trailhead, set among Pennsylvanian limestone cliffs, is 4 miles south of the traffic signal in the Village of Tijeras at an elevation of 6,800 feet. Walk down the gravel path from the parking lot. After the trailhead sign, the trail follows the surface of the former highway. Although it is paved, there may be gravel or twigs on the surface. Stop to check out the elm trees along both sides of the asphalt trail and scan the foliage on the cliffs.

Next, head to your right and follow the "Old Road" for about 0.25 mile, looking both in the shrubs in the arroyo and along the hillsides. Then double back to the dirt trail (#05056) that leads down into Otero Canyon. It is unmarked; the trail sign is back at the trailhead. Stop at the bottom of the slope to explore the trees along the trail. Keep to your right when the trail forks to go to the Cedro Creek Nature Trail, following the creek bed and ri-

Trail into Otero Canyon

parian habitat. After the monsoon rains arrive in midsummer, this area is alive with a variety of wildflowers.

The trail forks again after about half a mile. If you have not seen your target species, continue on Trail #05056 farther into Otero Canyon, staying alert for both mountain bikers and motorized dirt bikes. To see higher-elevation species, follow the well-marked Tunnel Spring Trail (#05145) to the right for a short distance. The Tunnel Spring Trail is narrow and has switchbacks up to the ridge. Since there are not many places for you to step off the trail, be alert for bicyclists. Ponderosa pines line both sides of the trail.

Before returning to the parking lot, you may also want to walk along the Cedro Creek Nature Trail, which is clearly marked at the first fork on the trail, where you will turn right. Mountain bikers are not allowed on this trail, which wanders for about a mile through Gambel oak hillsides and a riparian meadow before you have to turn around. The drawback to this trail is that it parallels the highway, and the noise of vehicles sometimes makes it difficult to hear bird calls, although this becomes less of a problem the farther you go.

Even though there are birds to be seen at any time of the year, the best time to bird this site is from mid-April through mid-September, early to midmorning.

County: Bernalillo

eBird Hotspot: Cedro Nature Trail

TARGET BIRDS

Red-naped and Williamson's Sapsuckers Either one is most frequently seen during fall (September–November) in the elm trees on both sides of the paved trail heading away from the parking area. Look for the sap wells in the bark.

Gray Flycatcher This is one of the few places where this species can be seen during nesting season in central New Mexico. It arrives mid-April and is present through August. Watch for it in the arroyo along the end of the old road or next to the trail through Otero Canyon.

Plumbeous Vireo This vireo also nests in the area. It may be seen along the arroyo bordering the paved trail and on either side of the nature trail starting in mid-April.

Townsend's Solitaire It can easily be spotted perched on top of ponderosa pines during the fall and winter.

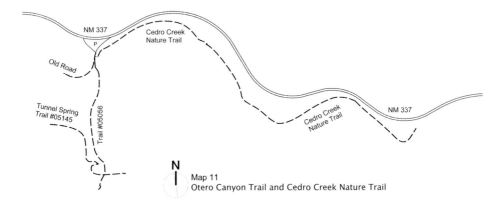

N

Map 11
Otero Canyon Trail and Cedro Creek Nature Trail

Black-throated Gray Warbler This is a prime nesting location for this species. Check along the arroyo bordering the paved trail and on either side of the nature trail, from the middle of April when it arrives from the tropics until mid- to late August when it heads south.

Townsend's Warbler This is a good location to see this warbler during fall migration, from mid-August through early October.

OTHER BIRDS

Birds that can be viewed year-round include Mountain Chickadee, Bewick's Wren, White-breasted Nuthatch, Northern Flicker, Bushtit, Juniper Titmouse, Spotted Towhee, American Robin, House Finch, and Brown-headed Cowbird.

During summer, check for Western Tanager in the ponderosa pines on the Tunnel Spring Trail; Virginia's Warbler along Trail #05056; and Cassin's Kingbird, Black-headed Grosbeak, Yellow-breasted Chat, and Western Wood-Pewee along the Cedro Nature Trail.

Fall and winter can bring Red-breasted Nuthatch, Mountain Bluebird, Cassin's Finch, Pine Siskin, Yellow-rumped Warbler, Dark-eyed Junco, Red Crossbill, and White-crowned Sparrow.

DIRECTIONS

By car: From the intersection of I-25 and I-40 in Albuquerque, drive east on I-40 approximately 14.5 miles to Exit 175, Tijeras (NM 337/NM 333). Immediately after you exit I-40, the ramp divides. Take the right fork, and merge

Red-naped Sapsucker (Photo by Bonnie L. Long)

onto NM 337. At the traffic light, continue south on NM 337 approximately 4 miles to the Otero Canyon trailhead parking area, which is on your right. Before you get to the Otero Canyon parking area, you will pass the Tunnel Canyon parking area, also on the right, approximately 3 miles from the traffic light. Drive slowly from this point, as the trailhead parking can be easy to miss. NM 337 then passes through a deep road cut. The Otero Canyon parking area will appear just after a fairly sharp curve to the left.

Public transportation: None available

PARKING

There is a small parking area at the trailhead. Because the parking area is right off the highway, it is recommended that you not leave valuables in the car.

None

- Poison ivy: Poison ivy sometimes grows along the edges of Cedro Creek. It is a bushier variety than poison ivy seen in the eastern United States. Look for the large green leaves in clusters of three (see photo in chapter 2).
- Rattlesnakes: Keep your eyes and ears alert for rattlesnakes during warm weather.
- Harvester ants: There are a multitude of anthills of this stinging insect on or near the trails.

- Accessibility: The dirt path leading from the parking lot would be too steep an incline for someone using a wheelchair. The old road beyond the dirt path is often strewn with debris. Trail #05056 has loose granite and a steep incline descending from the old road. Some prefer to use a walking stick to help prevent falls. All of the trails are single track.
- Restrooms: None available. The closest restroom is 3.3 miles north on NM-337 at the Sandia Ranger Station on weekdays or 2.9 miles south at the Pine Flat Picnic Area.
- Water: None available
- Picnic tables: None available

Several small restaurants, cafés, and bed-and-breakfast-style establishments are located 4 miles north in the Village of Tijeras along NM 333 (Historic Route 66). The nearest gas station is about 1 mile north of Tijeras. Go east on NM 333 from the intersection of NM 337 in Tijeras, and merge onto NM 14, heading north for 1 mile toward Cedar Crest. The nearest hotels are in Albuquerque at most exits along I-40 and I-25 beginning 8 miles west on I-40.

Tajique and Fourth of July Canyons

Located at the head of Tajique Canyon, 7 miles west of the village of Tajique, the Fourth of July Canyon's unique ecosystem has fostered the largest stand of Rocky Mountain and bigtooth maples in New Mexico. Luckily, one of the prime times of the year to go birding at this site corresponds with the brilliant red fall colors. The canyon, situated at 7,500 feet, comprises a transitional habitat of oak, piñon, and ponderosa pines, as well as the maples.

Tajique Canyon, which winds through several miles of burned forested area from a fire in the spring of 2008, has been designated by the National Audubon Society as an Important Bird Area because of the high numbers of breeding Virginia's and Grace's Warblers and Plumbeous Vireo. In addition, three other species of warblers breed in the area. Despite the burn, birds have returned to their traditional territories and are often easier to spot without the foliage.

Begin your birding as you drive west on the well-graded gravel road through Tajique Canyon (may be muddy after a rainstorm). Greater Road-runner and Western and Mountain Bluebirds are possible along the road. The currently unmarked Tajique Campground, which used to be an excellent place to stop, is temporarily closed due to fire and flood damage. A re-opening date is not yet available. Most of the birds are still present along the canyon.

Although you will see the typical high-forest bird species in the Fourth of July Campground area, to locate the area's specialties, take the Fourth of July Trail #173 or Spring Loop Trail (on the Mosca Campground Loop, the right fork after the pay station) into the canyon.

Fourth of July Campground usually closes in early November and re-opens sometime in April (weather dependent). When it is closed, visitors may park at the gate and hike in.

Return to NM 55 via the same route through Tajique Canyon.

County: Torrance

eBird Hotspot: Fourth of July Canyon

TARGET BIRDS

Plumbeous Vireo This high-altitude vireo is a summer resident. It arrives by mid-May and can be seen until the end of September.

Hermit Thrush It is a summer resident that nests in the low branches of small trees or bushes along Tajique Canyon Road, in the campground, and along the Fourth of July Trail from late spring through the end of July. After breeding season, look for it bobbing in the understory.

Fourth of July Canyon trailhead

Grace's Warbler It breeds high in the pines near and in the Fourth of July Campground.

Virginia's Warbler It is a summer resident and breeder. It arrives toward the end of April and stays through the end of August. It is found in the understory along Fourth of July Trail.

OTHER BIRDS

Year-round residents include Downy (Fourth of July) and Hairy Woodpeckers, Northern Flicker, Steller's Jay, Mountain Chickadee, Red-breasted and White-breasted Nuthatches, Brown Creeper, American Robin, Ruby-crowned Kinglet, and Pine Siskin. The nomadic Red Crossbill might also be found. Wild Turkey is a possibility in Fourth of July Canyon.

Summer residents and breeders include Broad-tailed Hummingbird;

Western Wood-Pewee; Cordilleran Flycatcher; Warbling and Plumbeous Vireos; Orange-crowned (Fourth of July), MacGillivray's, and Yellow-rumped (Audubon's) Warblers; and Black-headed Grosbeak.

During fall migration, look for Red-naped Sapsucker and Townsend's Warbler in Fourth of July Canyon and Olive-sided Flycatcher and Lazuli Bunting in Tajique Canyon.

DIRECTIONS

By car: From the intersection of I-25 and I-40 in Albuquerque, travel east on I-40 approximately 14.5 miles to Exit 175, Tijeras (NM 337/NM 333). At Tijeras, drive south on NM 337 for 29 miles to a T intersection, and then turn right. Follow NM 55 for approximately 3 miles to the village of Tajique. In Tajique, look for the cylindrical water tower on your right. Turn right just before the water tower on County Road A013 (Forest Route 55), which is gravel, and travel west 7.1 miles, following the periodic campground signs along the way to an intersecting road on the right. Turn right (campground sign will be visible after turn) into campground.

Public transportation: None available

PARKING

There is parking before the restrooms and pay station or in the day-use area.

FEES

There are no fees for parking in the day-use area. There is an $8.00 daily fee for camping.

SPECIAL CONSIDERATIONS AND HAZARDS

■ Bears: Bears are possible at this location. Do not leave any food on a picnic table, even for a short period of time while you walk away to bird. Refer to safety guidelines in chapter 2.

■ Cougars: There have been cougar sightings in this area. Refer to safety guidelines in chapter 2.

FACILITIES

■ Accessibility: There is a wheelchair-accessible restroom near the entrance. The Fourth of July Canyon Trail is single track and fairly level for about 0.25 mile.

- Restrooms: Available in the entrance parking area and in the campgrounds
- Water: None available
- Picnic tables: There are tables in the day use-picnic area.

FOOD, GAS, AND LODGING

The nearest food, gas, and lodging are available 21.5 miles south on NM 55 at the town of Mountainair. Bed-and-breakfast lodging is available in the village of Tajique.

Capilla Peak and Manzano HawkWatch

DESCRIPTION

Capilla Peak, at an elevation of 9,200 feet, is located on the Rocky Mountain branch of the Central Flyway and has been designated by Audubon New Mexico as an Important Bird Area. HawkWatch International volunteers count and band hawks on the ridge between August 25 and November 5. The peak period is the last week in September and first two weeks in October.

As many as 18 different species of raptors have been seen during a banding season. An educator is sometimes on-site on weekends, and often during the week, to answer questions. The public is welcome to visit at any time. Many people find it helpful to download the flight silhouettes from the HawkWatch Web site (www.hawkwatch.org/news-and-events/330-hmana). The trail to the Capilla Peak observation site starts just before the entrance to Capilla Peak Campground. Hike the 1-mile Gavilan Trail (marked with a hawk silhouette) to reach the observation point.

Rio Grande Bird Research is studying the smaller birds that utilize the high-altitude habitat of ponderosa pine, aspen, oak, and fir during fall migration. They band on Mondays from the third week in August through the end of October. They set up their operation at the base of the fire watch tower in the parking area at the entrance to Capilla Peak Campground. This is also an area where high-mountain birds breed during the summer.

County: Torrance

eBird Hotspot: Cibola NF—Capilla Peak

TARGET BIRDS

Sharp-shinned and Cooper's Hawks Both of these hawks can be spotted here during September and October. Most years these are the most common raptors. You will have ample opportunities to learn to differentiate between these two species.

Swainson's Hawk This is another prevalent raptor that migrates over the HawkWatch site; however, numbers vary tremendously from year to year.

Red-tailed Hawk This hawk is a year-round resident in central New Mexico, but many arrive to winter in the area, while others continue over the Manzano Mountains as they head farther south. It is frequently observed at the HawkWatch count site.

Golden Eagle One or two might be seen on any given day over the ridge. It is most frequently seen during October.

Lewis's Woodpecker Although it is a year-round resident in the northern part of the state, it also migrates to the mountains in southern New Mexico and has been spotted by HawkWatch volunteers while counting raptors.

Golden-crowned and Ruby-crowned Kinglets These two species nest in the high spruce-fir forests. The Ruby-crowned is the most prevalent of all the birds banded in the area below the ridge.

Williamson's Sapsucker held by Master Bander Steve Cox at Capilla Peak (Photo by Laurel Eloise Ladwig)

Other raptors normally spotted from the ridge at some point during migration include Northern Goshawk, Broad-winged and Ferruginous Hawks, American Kestrel, Merlin, and Peregrine Falcon. Seen less frequently are Rough-legged Hawk, Bald Eagle, and Prairie Falcon. In addition, migrating and local Band-tailed Pigeon is often spotted at the HawkWatch site.

Migrants below the ridge include Williamson's Sapsucker (mid-August–September); Hammond's and Dusky Flycatchers (end of August and first week in September); Cassin's Vireo (August and September); Hermit Thrush (primarily September and early October); and Orange-crowned, Townsend's, MacGillivray's and Wilson's Warblers (end of August through mid-September).

Year-round birds include Northern Flicker, Steller's Jay, Mountain Chickadee, Red-breasted Nuthatch, and Brown Creeper.

DIRECTIONS

By car: The site is accessed by a 9-mile dirt road that heads west from the village of Manzano on Forest Road 245, the first right just opposite the church. The road travels through the burn area from the Trigo fire during the spring of 2008. Follow the signs for New Canyon and Capilla Peak Campgrounds, which continue to be closed (as of August 2010) due to fire damage. The road is deeply rutted, has intermittent streams running across it, is extremely muddy after rainstorms, and is accessible only with a high-clearance or four-wheel-drive vehicle. The road beyond New Canyon Campground continues to be closed, so it is wise to call both HawkWatch in Albuquerque (505-255-7622) and the Mountainair District Ranger Station (505-847-2990) for the latest conditions.

Public transportation: None available

PARKING

Park along the road near the trailhead or at the parking lot at the base of the fire watch tower.

FEES

There is a $5.00 camping fee when the campgrounds reopen.

SPECIAL CONSIDERATIONS AND HAZARDS

- Bears: They often frequent campgrounds in this area. Refer to safety guidelines in chapter 2.
- Remote area: Because this is a remote area, it is important to bring adequate food and water.
- Altitude: Because this site is at an elevation of 9,200 feet, the effects of altitude are important to remember. See information on altitude in chapter 2. The temperature can be as much as 20°F cooler than that in Mountainair or Albuquerque. Warm clothes and rain gear are essential.

FACILITIES

- Accessibility: The trail to Capilla Peak is single track, extremely rocky, and steep.
- Restrooms: Available at New Canyon and Capilla Peak Campgrounds when they reopen
- Water: None available
- Picnic tables: Available at New Canyon and Capilla Peak Campgrounds when they reopen

FOOD, GAS, AND LODGING

The nearest food, gas, and lodging are available 24.7 miles south on NM 55 at the town of Mountainair. Bed-and-breakfast lodging is available north on NM 55 in the village of Tajique.

Salinas Pueblo Missions National Monument–Quarai Unit

DESCRIPTION

At an elevation of 6,600 feet, situated in the Manzano Mountains in Torrance County, the Quarai Unit of the Salinas Pueblo Missions National Monument provides an opportunity to visit the ruins of an ancient pueblo dating from the 1300s. Comprising both riparian and piñon-juniper habitats supporting diverse species of nesting birds, it is a prime location during spring and fall migrations and hosts International Migratory Bird Day activities.

Begin birding as you drive along the access road from NM 55. Once in the parking lot, search the trees and bushes along the park boundary. At the Quarai Contact Station, you can pick up a brochure and map, visit the small museum, or browse the bookstore. Start your tour of the grounds by heading along the trail that leads from the Contact Station toward the ruins of the church and *convento* (old Spanish word, referring to the ruins of living quarters, designated on the trail map), checking out the foliage growing around the ruins to your right closer to the *convento*.

The ruins themselves can be productive. Say's Phoebe, swallows, and sometimes Rock Wren nest there. The resident Great Horned Owl often can be found perched in one of the niches.

The trail leads past the ruins. Before turning right on the path, take a few moments to bird the scrub just beyond. Then follow the trail toward the cottonwood grove and spring-fed arroyo, checking the fruit-bearing bushes, including chokecherry and gooseberry, and listening for the call of a Yellow-breasted Chat. Just beyond a small footbridge, pause to inspect the foliage around a tiny pond. As you walk left along the route, scan the cottonwoods that grow along the creek.

The trail continues slightly uphill to the piñon-juniper habitat and then turns right across the uplands until it drops back down to the cottonwood grove, where the picnic area is located. It is definitely worthwhile to take a picnic lunch, as many species can be spotted flitting in the branches of the cottonwoods while you eat.

The park is open daily 9:00 A.M.–6:00 P.M. from Memorial Day through Labor Day, and 9:00 A.M.–5:00 P.M. during the rest of the year.

County: Torrance

eBird Hotspot: Quarai Ruins Salinas NM

Web site for more information: www.nps.gov/sapu/index.htm

TARGET BIRDS

Great Horned Owl It is a year-round resident and breeder and has been known to nest or perch in the *convento* ruins. If you do not spot one there, search the large branches of the cottonwood trees. May is a good month to see fledglings.

Ladder-backed Woodpecker It is a year-round resident; however, it sometimes is difficult to see since it tends to rove around to glean for insects.

Cassin's Kingbird This species of kingbird is the most prevalent at this elevation. It is a summer resident often seen near the road leading into the monument.

Plumbeous and Warbling Vireos Although both vireos can be spotted, the Plumbeous Vireo is more common. The Plumbeous nests at the monument, while the Warbling is seen only during migration. Look for either of them in the riparian area, especially near the small pond or in the cottonwoods.

Great Horned Owl in *convento*

Violet-green Swallow It is a summer resident, arriving at the end of March. Throughout the breeding season, you can see it swooping in and out of the *convento* ruins. It nests in the spaces between the bricks of the *convento*, both on the interior and exterior walls.

Juniper Titmouse It is a year-round resident. Listen for its buzzy call in the piñon pines on the upland part of the trail.

Mountain Bluebird This species of bluebird is a summer resident and nests in the area. While it might be spotted at any time of the year, search for it at the spring along the road leading into the monument or in the trees east of the ruins. It occasionally nests in the *convento*.

Phainopepla Although not prevalent, it is a summer resident. It arrives in June, later than the other nesting species, and can be seen through August. Look for it in the trees along the west side of the monument and parking area.

Yellow-breasted Chat It is a summer resident and breeder. The riparian area along the creek often harbors a number of chats. Listen for its distinctive call to locate one in the dense foliage, but be aware that its varied chattering often resembles the sounds of several other birds.

OTHER BIRDS

Year-round birds include Mourning, White-winged, and Eurasian Collared-Doves; Northern Flicker; Say's Phoebe; Western Scrub-Jay; Bushtit; Bewick's Wren; American Robin; Spotted Towhee; and House Finch. On the access road you might see Western Meadowlark and possibly Pinyon Jay.

Birds that are summer residents and breeders include Black-chinned and Broad-tailed Hummingbirds, Western Wood-Pewee, Ash-throated Flycatcher, Barn Swallow, Rock Wren, Northern Mockingbird, Virginia's Warbler, Western Tanager, Chipping and Lark Sparrows, Black-headed and Blue Grosbeaks, Lazuli Bunting, and Bullock's Oriole. Turkey Vulture and Swainson's Hawk can be seen in the thermals over the monument. In some years, Gray Flycatcher nests at the monument.

During migration look for Olive-sided, Dusky, and Gray Flycatchers; Cassin's Vireo; House Wren; Cedar Waxwing; Orange-crowned, Yellow, Yellow-rumped, MacGillivray's, and Wilson's Warblers; Northern Waterthrush; Common Yellowthroat; Summer Tanager; and Green-tailed Towhee. Every year a number of eastern strays are spotted during migration.

During winter White-crowned and Song Sparrows, Dark-eyed Junco, and occasionally Marsh Wren and Cassin's Finch join the year-round birds.

DIRECTIONS

By car: Start from the intersection of I-25 and I-40 in Albuquerque, and travel east on I-40 approximately 15 miles to Exit 175, Tijeras (NM 337/NM 333). At Tijeras, travel 29 miles south on NM 337 to a T intersection and turn right. Follow NM 55 for approximately 17 miles to signs for

Salinas Pueblo Missions National Monument. Turn right, driving 1 mile west to Quarai Unit (approximately a 2-hour drive).

Public transportation: None available

PARKING
There is a large parking lot, including wheelchair-accessible spaces.

FEES
None

SPECIAL CONSIDERATIONS AND HAZARDS
- Rattlesnakes: There is the possibility of rattlesnakes during warm weather.
- Mosquitoes: During the summer, particularly after rainstorms, there are mosquitoes near the chokeberry bushes, in the area of the stream, and sometimes in the picnic area.

FACILITIES
- Accessibility: The path to the church and *convento* is packed gravel. The trail that leads to the riparian area is dirt and fairly level. The trail up through the piñon-juniper habitat is narrow and uneven.
- Restrooms: Restrooms are located on the side of the Contact Station and include a wheelchair-accessible stall.
- Water: There is a drinking fountain next to the restrooms.
- Picnic tables: Picnic tables are available along a path south of the Contact Station.

FOOD, GAS, AND LODGING
The nearest food, gas, and lodging are available 8 miles south on NM 55 at the town of Mountainair. Bed-and-breakfast lodging is available 15 miles north in the village of Tajique on NM 55.

CHAPTER 7

Petroglyph National Monument

General Overview

The edge of the lava flow formed by now-extinct volcanic activity creates a long, narrow corridor of 7,244 acres on Albuquerque's West Mesa and is preserved in Petroglyph National Monument. The basalt escarpment and dunelike sands produce a unique environment for plants and other wildlife. Several trailheads lead into the monument, two of which are described here, Rinconada Canyon on the southern end and Piedras Marcadas on the northern end. The area is managed in a partnership with Albuquerque Open Space, which maintains two of the trailheads, including Piedras Marcadas.

A visit to Petroglyph National Monument is enhanced by stopping first at Las Imagenes Visitor Center, located off Unser Boulevard NW (NM 345) on Western Trail Road NW (3 miles north of I-40).

Directions to the sites in the Petroglyph National Monument can be found in the individual site descriptions.

Rinconada Canyon

DESCRIPTION

Located at the south end of the Petroglyph National Monument at an elevation of 5,200 feet, Rinconada Canyon Trail is one of Albuquerque West Mesa's most popular locations for hiking and viewing ancient Native American petroglyphs (images hewn into the rock). The trail traverses sand dunes, winding through an eroded canyon at the edge of a basaltic lava flow originating from five extinct volcanoes.

From the parking lot, the trail heads west for a short distance and then forks. The trail loops around, so you can start on either segment. The right-

Petroglyph of quail

hand fork leads along the base of the escarpment covered with basalt boulders and provides the opportunity to view both Canyon and Rock Wrens and Rufous-crowned Sparrow. The side trails to specific petroglyphs offer additional opportunities to venture into small canyons.

At the far western end, the trail loops south and then back toward the parking lot. Before making the return trip, take a moment to scan overhead for raptors, which often can be seen circling over the lava escarpment or perching on power poles. This part of the trail crosses sandy dunes, bordered by sand sage, four-wing saltbush, and broom snakeweed, prime hiding places for a variety of birds.

Before you hike the canyon, it may be useful to visit the Visitor Center (open 8:00 A.M.–5:00 P.M.; closed Thanksgiving Day, Christmas Day, and New Year's Day), located farther north along Unser Boulevard, to obtain current information.

County: Bernalillo
eBird Hotspot: Petroglyphs NM—Rinconada Canyon
Web site for more information and map: www.nps.gov/petr/planyour
visit/rincon.htm

Scaled Quail It is a year-round resident and breeder. During breeding season, the male may perch on top of a large bush or rock outcropping and call to protect his territory. At other times of the year, it is harder to find; you might come across a small covey scooting from the shelter of one bush to another.

Greater Roadrunner The roadrunner is a year-round resident. One or two Greater Roadrunners are often seen in this canyon.

Loggerhead Shrike It is a year-round resident and breeder. It used to be more prevalent, but its numbers are declining as development encroaches on the monument. Often one can be spotted in the canyon flatlands about 50 yards west of the parking lot and at the far end of the trail. Loggerhead Shrikes like to perch on wires, which provide an expansive view of the scrub, while searching for food.

Rock and Canyon Wrens They are year-round residents and breeders. Canyon Wren is often heard trilling from the canyon walls but is much harder to observe. Look for Rock Wren bobbing on the boulders.

Crissal Thrasher It is the only thrasher that breeds in the monument.

Rufous-crowned Sparrow It is a year-round resident and breeder that forages on the ground and under bushes, making it difficult to find. Its plumage can be camouflaged by the rocks.

Black-throated Sparrow It is present from early March through September, and sometimes later. It can be seen easily during breeding season when the male often sings visibly from a four-wing saltbush. After breeding season, it tends to stay hidden in the bushes. Watch and listen for its activity; it often responds to pishing.

Sage Sparrow The Petroglyph National Monument is about the only reliable location in Albuquerque to see a Sage Sparrow. It arrives mid-October and stays until mid- to late March. Look for it on the ground or when it appears briefly on top of a bush. It holds its tail high when it runs and flicks it downward when perched.

The target birds are the principal species seen. Others are present in lesser numbers.

A variety of individual raptors have been viewed circling over Rinconada Canyon at different times of the year, including Turkey Vulture (summer), Cooper's Hawk (year-round), Swainson's Hawk (summer), Red-tailed Hawk (year-round), and American Kestrel (year-round).

Year-round birds include Great Horned Owl, Mourning Dove, Common Raven, Say's Phoebe, Bewick's Wren, Curve-billed Thrasher (occasional visitor), Canyon Towhee, Eastern and Western Meadowlarks (on the top of the mesa), Lesser Goldfinch, and House Finch.

During migration, Blue-gray Gnatcatcher actively forages in the saltbush as it works its way south in the fall. Hermit Thrush, Green-tailed Towhee, and Vesper and Brewer's Sparrows are regularly seen during fall migration.

Possible summer residents are Common Nighthawk, Barn Swallow, Northern Mockingbird, Cassin's and Western Kingbirds, and Black-chinned Hummingbird.

Winter residents include White-crowned Sparrow and Dark-eyed (Oregon) Junco. Sage Thrasher sometimes is seen during the winter months.

DIRECTIONS

By car: From the intersection of I-25 and I-40 in Albuquerque, travel west on I-40 approximately 5.5 miles to Exit 154, Unser Boulevard NW (NM 345). Turn north (right) on Unser, and drive 2.5 miles to St. Joseph's Avenue NW. Turn left into the parking lot for Rinconada Canyon trailhead. The Petroglyph National Monument Visitor Center is 1 mile farther north on Unser Boulevard NW. Turn left at Western Trail NW, and follow it to the end.

Public transportation: None available

PARKING

There is a roomy, paved parking area off Unser Boulevard NW. Note: This parking area has experienced vehicle break-ins. Do not leave any valuables in your car.

FEES

None

- Rattlesnakes: Two species of rattlesnakes reside in the canyon. Be alert for them on both the rocks and the sand during warm weather.
- Environmental fragility: Rinconada Canyon has a fragile ecosystem. It is important to remain on the trails. The area is protected under the Archaeological Resources Protection Act.

FACILITIES

- Accessibility: The parking lot is paved. The trail is narrow, often uneven, and crosses sand dunes.
- Restrooms: A wheelchair-accessible restroom is located at the trailhead.
- Water: None available. There is a drinking fountain at the Visitor Center (1 mile north).
- Picnic tables: Picnic tables are available near the parking lot.

FOOD, GAS, AND LODGING

There are fast-food restaurants and gas stations approximately 1.5 miles south of Rinconada Canyon at Unser Boulevard NW and Vista Oriente Street (98th Street NW). There is a bed-and-breakfast establishment nearby, and numerous hotels are located at Exit 155, about 1 mile east of Unser Boulevard NW on I-40 at Coors Boulevard NW (NM 448).

Piedras Marcadas

DESCRIPTION

Piedras Marcadas (marked rocks) Canyon is located on the northern edge of Petroglyph National Monument and is tucked behind a residential area. Although you can see the backs of the houses that border the national monument lands, the area provides surprisingly good birding and tends to be less crowded than Rinconada Canyon. The 1.8-mile trail follows the base of a basalt escarpment and detours into several small canyons. The trailhead is maintained by the City of Albuquerque Open Space Division. A sign at the edge of the parking area provides a generalized trail map and other visitor information. A site bulletin is available at the Petroglyph National Monument Visitor Center. (See Rinconada Canyon site for directions.)

Start your exploration by walking along the path that leads to the boundary of the national monument. Check any feeders in the yards of the

Trail into Piedras Marcadas

houses that border the trail. Please respect their privacy. Go through the formal entrance rather than around the right-hand side of the boundary. It is a good idea to study the interpretive trailhead sign to help you visualize your route. When you reach a gate that provides entrance for emergency vehicles, enter through the opening on the left-hand side of the barrier. The trail then leads down a sandy fire road, which narrows as it enters the canyon. As you walk along the trail, follow the arrows leading to numbered petroglyphs, which also help you cover all of the area. When you get to #6, turn around and head back, this time staying on the main path. As in Rinconada Canyon, the trail is bordered by sand sage, four-wing saltbush, and broom snakeweed.

County: Bernalillo

eBird Hotspot: Petroglyphs NM—Piedras Marcadas

Web site for more information and map: www.nps.gov/petr/planyour visit/pmc.htm

TARGET BIRDS

Scaled Quail This quail is a year-round resident and breeder. During breeding season, the male may perch on a bush or rock outcropping and call to protect his territory. At other times of the year, it is harder to find; you might come across a small covey scooting from the cover of one bush to another. Gambel's Quail is starting to be seen at Piedras Marcadas as well, but in very small numbers.

Great Horned Owl It is a year-round resident that nests among the basalt boulders. Check for it on the ridge or partway down the escarpment at dusk or dawn.

Crissal Thrasher This is a particularly good location for Crissal Thrasher, which breeds here. Listen for its distinctive call. It prefers dense shrubs.

Canyon Towhee It is a year-round resident and breeder that often can be seen scurrying across the trail.

Sage Sparrow A few spend the winter at this location. This sparrow arrives mid-October and stays until mid- to late March. Look for it foraging under the bushes or popping up briefly. It can be distinguished from other winter sparrows by its tail—held high when running and flicking downward when perched.

OTHER BIRDS

Year-round birds include Cooper's Hawk, White-winged and Mourning Doves, Greater Roadrunner, Say's Phoebe, Rock and Bewick's Wrens, Black-throated Sparrow, Western Meadowlark, House Finch, Lesser Goldfinch, and Common Raven. Curve-billed Thrasher may forage here but does not breed at this location because there is no cholla cactus, its preferred nesting site.

Winter residents include Sharp-shinned Hawk, Northern Harrier, White-crowned Sparrow, and Dark-eyed (Oregon) Junco.

Summer residents include Turkey Vulture, Common Nighthawk, Black-chinned Hummingbird, Cassin's and Western Kingbirds, Barn Swallow, and Northern Mockingbird.

Birds possible during migration include Blue-gray Gnatcatcher, Sage Thrasher, Green-tailed Towhee, and Chipping and Vesper Sparrows.

By car: From the intersection of I-40 and I-25 in Albuquerque, travel north on I-25 for 5.8 miles to Exit 232, Paseo del Norte Boulevard (NM 423). At the off-ramp, turn left and follow Paseo del Norte west for 6 miles (keep left after crossing the bridge over the Rio Grande). Turn right on Golf Course Road NW, and drive 0.6 mile to Jill Patricia Street NW. Turn left. The Piedras Marcadas parking lot will be 0.1 mile on the right.

Public transportation: Albuquerque city bus 157 stops at Paseo del Norte and Golf Course Road NW. Walk north on Golf Course Road NW for 0.6 mile to Jill Patricia Street NW. Turn left. The trailhead parking lot will be on your right. See "Public Transportation" section in chapter 2 for more information.

PARKING

There is a small paved parking lot.

FEES

None

SPECIAL CONSIDERATIONS AND HAZARDS

- Rattlesnakes: Keep your eyes and ears alert for rattlesnakes during warm weather.
- Environmental fragility: The area has a fragile ecosystem. It is important to remain on the trails. The area is protected under the Archaeological Resources Protection Act.

FACILITIES

- Accessibility: Although the trailhead area is wheelchair accessible, the trail is paved only up to the boundary of the park. The rest of the trail is single track, often uneven, and crosses sand dunes.
- Restrooms: None available. The closest restroom is in a fast-food restaurant near the intersection of Jill Patricia Street NW and Golf Course Road NW.
- Water: None available
- Picnic tables: There are picnic tables in the park near a different entrance off Tia Christina Drive NW. This entrance can be accessed

by driving beyond the parking area on Jill Patricia Street NW to the intersection with Tia Christina Drive NW. The Tia Christina park entrance is on the right.

There are numerous restaurants and gas stations throughout Albuquerque. Lodging is concentrated at most exits along I-25 and I-40, as well as near the intersection of Jill Patricia Street NW and Golf Course Road NW.

CHAPTER 8

South of Albuquerque

General Overview

This area features five site descriptions, also part of the middle Rio Grande, that follow the Rio Grande south of Albuquerque to the Bosque del Apache National Wildlife Refuge. I-25 follows not only the river but also the historic El Camino Real de Tierra Adentro (the Royal Road of Interior Lands), which the Spanish conquistadors began to use at the end of the sixteenth century. The area is dotted with rural communities, each with a rich cultural heritage.

The bosque at River Park in Los Lunas is bordered by the Rio Grande on the west and agricultural fields on the east, providing a wide array of birds. There are two sites in Belen: the Belen Marsh, not too far from the interstate; and Whitfield Wildlife Conservation Area (WCA), surrounded by agricultural fields and the Rio Grande bosque along its western edge. A little farther south, the Bernardo Wildlife Management Area (WMA) is nestled between the interstate and the river and includes a working farm that produces crops for migrating birds. Farthest south is Bosque del Apache National Wildlife Refuge, known for its wintering Sandhill Cranes and Snow Geese.

General Directions

The sites in this section all can be accessed from I-25 by traveling south from the intersection of I-40 and I-25 in Albuquerque. Exit 203 off I-25, about 23 miles south of the city, leads to Main Street for Los Lunas River Park. Exit 195, approximately 30.5 miles south of Albuquerque at Belen, leads to both Belen Marsh and Whitfield Wildlife Conservation Area. Exit 175, about 51 miles south of Albuquerque, is the exit for Bernardo Wildlife Management Area. Exit 139 is the exit for Bosque del Apache at the turn to San Antonio, approximately 87 miles south of the city. Detailed directions can found in the descriptions for the individual sites.

Los Lunas River Park

DESCRIPTION

River Park is a semideveloped site, shaded by large cottonwood trees, along the east side of the Rio Grande right off Main Street in the town of Los Lunas. A packed gravel trail leads from the parking lot through the bosque to the river and then loops north and back to the starting point. Just before the trail reaches the river, take a detour on an informal path that leads south for a short way. Once at the river, wander out to the edge to investigate the small trees and shrubs on either side, as well as the sandbars.

After completing the loop and returning to the parking lot, continue over to the levee along the irrigation ditch. There are steps allowing you to go up and walk along the levee. During the winter, check the fields for possible foraging Sandhill Cranes and Snow Geese. If they are not visible, you can make a side trip along nearby Edeal Road to look for them in other fields. (See "Directions" for more specific instructions.)

County: Valencia

eBird Hotspot: Los Lunas River Park

TARGET BIRDS

Mississippi Kite Although Mississippi Kite has been seen at various locations along the middle Rio Grande, River Park has been a documented nesting site and a key location for viewing it throughout the summer. It arrives in early May and departs by mid-September.

Cliff Swallow It is a summer resident that arrives in early May and is gone by the end of August. It nests in colonies under the Main Street bridge over the Rio Grande.

Summer Tanager It is a summer resident and nests in the cottonwood trees.

Black-headed Grosbeak It also is a summer resident nesting in the cottonwoods

Birders at River Park

OTHER BIRDS

Year-round birds include Mallard, Ring-necked Pheasant, Cooper's Hawk, American Kestrel, Mourning Dove, Greater Roadrunner, Downy Woodpecker, Northern Flicker, Black and Say's Phoebes, American Crow, Black-capped Chickadee, White-breasted Nuthatch, Bewick's Wren, Spotted Towhee, and House Finch.

Summer residents include Snowy Egret, Turkey Vulture, Black-chinned Hummingbird, Western Kingbird, Cliff and Barn Swallows, and Blue Grosbeak.

Fall and winter residents include Red-tailed Hawk, Ruby-crowned Kinglet, Song and White-crowned Sparrows, and Dark-eyed Junco. Look for American Pipits and Red-winged Blackbirds in the plowed fields east of the levee. Sandhill Cranes sometimes have been observed on a sandbar in the river, as well as foraging in the fields.

Birds possible to see during spring and fall migration are Violet-green and Northern Rough-winged Swallows; a variety of migrating flycatchers; Yellow-rumped and Wilson's Warblers, as well as other western migrating warblers; Western Tanager; and Chipping Sparrow.

DIRECTIONS
By car: From the intersection of I-40 and I-25 in Albuquerque, travel south for approximately 23 miles on I-25 to Exit 203, Los Lunas. Turn left (east) onto NM 6 (Main Street), and travel approximately 3 miles through the town of Los Lunas. River Park will be on the right, just after crossing the low bridge over the Rio Grande.

After completing your visit during the winter months, you might want to turn right on NM 6 and then take the first right on Edeal Road (0.1 mile from River Park and Main Street to Edeal Road), checking the fields along the road for Sandhill Cranes and Snow Geese. After 2.4 miles at the ditch crossing, turn around and retrace your route to Main Street.

Public transportation: None available

PARKING
There is a large parking area.

FEES
None

SPECIAL CONSIDERATIONS AND HAZARDS
- Chiggers: They may be present in the grassy areas near the nature trails during warm weather. To help prevent the mite larvae from attaching themselves, tuck your pant legs into your socks.
- Mosquitoes: You might encounter mosquitoes on the trail near the river during the summer rainy season.

FACILITIES
- Accessibility: The trail to the river is level, packed gravel. The stairs to the levee area do not have handrails. The top of the levee has an even surface.
- Restrooms: Restrooms are available, and one is wheelchair accessible.

- Water: None available
- Picnic tables: Picnic tables are available, and a few are covered.

There are numerous restaurants less than 1 mile east or west of the park along Main Street in Los Lunas. Gas is available in Los Lunas. The nearest lodging is less than 0.25 mile east on Main Street or 3 miles west at Exit 203 off I-25.

Belen Marsh

DESCRIPTION

The Belen Marsh is an "accidental" gem just off the I-25 Bypass in the town of Belen. Located across from Walmart and Taco Bell, it has been known to birders as the "Taco Bell Marsh." The water table in the area is very near the surface. When dirt was removed for highway construction in the 1980s, the depression began to fill with water and a marsh habitat was established. It has become a wintering home to waterfowl, a summer breeding area for large waders and summer waterfowl, and an important stopover for migrating shorebirds.

Start your visit by quietly walking along the dirt road just behind Taco Bell, scanning the prairie dog mounds for summering Burrowing Owl (March–September).

Birding at the marsh must be done from the edge of Don Felipe Road, which is often busy with traffic. The marsh property owners request that birders and others stay off the property itself.

One to two hours before sundown is the best time to visit at any time of the year. The sun will be at your back, and the birds are actively feeding and flying in to roost for the night.

It is worth checking the area between the highway and the pond, and the fields and undeveloped areas south of the pond and along Sunset Road (opposite the middle of the pond).

County: Valencia

eBird Hotspot: Belen (Taco Bell) Marsh

TARGET BIRDS

Snowy and Cattle Egrets Although there is no rookery at this site, nonnesting egrets of both species roost here. Snowy Egret begins arriving at the end of

Black-necked Stilt along edge of marsh

March, and Cattle Egret arrives in April. They are both gone by the end of September.

White-faced Ibis This is an important migrant stopover for ibis. One or two begin arriving in February; however, most visit during March and April. They begin arriving at the end of July for their southward migration, with the greatest numbers in August and September. Be sure to check the flocks; sometimes there is a Glossy Ibis traveling with them.

Black-necked Stilt Numerous pairs nest here. They begin arriving in mid-March and are gone by the end of August.

American Avocet One or two pairs consistently nest here, arriving in early April. They are gone by the end of August.

Burrowing Owl This owl often nests in the vacant lot behind Taco Bell or on the south side of Sunset Road about halfway down the block. It arrives by mid-March and leaves by the end of September.

Chihuahuan Raven While not very prevalent, both Common and Chihuahuan Ravens have been observed at this site. Look around the fast-food restaurant, where it may be scavenging.

Year-round residents and breeders include Mallard, Ruddy Duck, Pied-billed Grebe, American Coot, Killdeer, Red-winged Blackbird, Great-tailed Grackle, and Western Meadowlark. Also seen at any time of the year are Black and Say's Phoebes.

Regular winter residents include Gadwall, Northern Shoveler, and Green-winged Teal. Brewer's Blackbird often roosts here, and Marsh Wren sometimes can be heard calling.

Blue-winged and Cinnamon Teal are summer residents and breeders. Barn, Cliff, and Northern Rough-winged Swallows frequently are seen during the summer, particularly at dusk. If they are not swooping over the pond, look for them perched on power lines along the road. Black-chinned Hummingbird and Western Kingbird can be spotted. Listen for Virginia Rail and Common Yellowthroat in the reeds. Both probably breed here.

Migrants that regularly stop over at the Belen Marsh both northbound and southbound include Franklin's Gull; Wilson's Phalarope; Long-billed Dowitcher; Spotted, Western, Least, and Baird's Sandpipers; Violet-green Swallow; and Yellow-headed Blackbird. In addition, there are several species that visit only during fall migration: Solitary and Stilt Sandpipers, Lesser Yellowlegs, and Sora.

DIRECTIONS

By car: From the intersection of I-25 and I-40 in Albuquerque, drive south on I-25 approximately 30 miles to Exit 195, Belen. Travel east on the I-25 Bypass for approximately 1.5 miles to Taco Bell. Turn right on Don Felipe Road. The marsh will be on the left.

Public transportation: None available

PARKING

Parking is almost nonexistent. It is important to park sufficiently off the road so as not to impede transportation along Don Felipe Road. Please do not block private businesses. Many birders park at the fast-food restaurant and patronize the business to express their appreciation.

None

- Traffic: Because there is no adequate place to stand, vehicles on Don Felipe Road can be a risk.
- Mosquitoes: The high water table encourages mosquito breeding in the adjacent fields. The marsh itself is regularly treated with a non-toxic bacillus.

FACILITIES

- Accessibility: The shoulders of the road are narrow and uneven.
- Restrooms: Restrooms are available in the fast-food restaurant (after it opens at 10:00 A.M.) or across the street at a mini-mart.
- Water: Bottled water can be purchased at the fast-food restaurant or across the street at the mini-mart.
- Picnic tables: None available

FOOD, GAS, AND LODGING

Hotels are located on I-25 at Exit 191 (the next exit south). Gas stations and restaurants, in addition to Taco Bell, are available along Main Street in Belen. Travel east on I-25 Bypass until it merges with North Main Street (NM 314), going south through the center of town.

Whitfield Wildlife Conservation Area

DESCRIPTION

Covering 100 acres, the Whitfield Wildlife Conservation Area in the town of Belen is a relatively new wildlife area. Owned and managed by the Valencia County Soil and Water Conservation District, it includes a variety of habitats composed of riparian cottonwood area, open meadow and grasslands, and a wetland. Volunteers have planted over 3,000 trees, such as cottonwood, screwbean mesquite, Goodding's willow, and New Mexico olive.

Start your visit at the Visitor Center. There are displays, and binoculars and field guides are available for loan. Future plans in the next phase of construction include a gift shop.

Next, follow the trail down to the wetlands, keeping to your right. A variety of waterbirds may be encountered plying the pond and seasonally flooded

Wetlands

fields. Just beyond the wetlands is a grassy area being restored as a salt grass marsh, possible due to the high alkalinity of the groundwater. On your right is an area planted with crops such as milo and corn. As you walk farther on the path, you will enter an area of recently planted trees mingled with old-growth cottonwoods.

When the trail reaches the west end of the conservation area, it heads south along a buffer zone adjacent to the Rio Grande. Currently there is no access to the bosque. There is a break in the fence to allow people access to the ditch bank and the riverside drain. When you reach the trail running along the south side of the property, turn left and make your way back to the entrance. The access to the path that leads to the break in the fence is from this path, which runs along the south property line.

Three moist soil units (areas planted in the spring and then flooded in the fall) provide habitat for wintering cranes on the south side of the conservation area. There is also a pollinator garden.

The Visitor Center is open Fridays and Saturdays from 8:00 A.M. to 2:00 P.M. and other times by appointment for special groups, such as school classes and birding tours. The grounds are open dawn to dusk 365 days a year.

County: Valencia

eBird Hotspot: Whitfield Wildlife Conservation Area

Web site for additional information: www.whitfieldwildlife.org

TARGET BIRDS

Bald Eagle In winter, Bald Eagle migrates to this area of the Rio Grande valley and has been reported spending as long as a month or so at Whitfield in late winter. Look for it in the large cottonwoods on the southwest side of the refuge.

White-faced Ibis The wildlife area's wetland is a stopover during both spring and fall migrations. Many stay through the summer at Whitfield. Be sure to check the flocks for an occasional Glossy Ibis.

Sandhill Crane This crane winters in the middle Rio Grande valley and can be found foraging in the fields and grassy area between the pond and the river. It may roost at night in the wetlands at Whitfield.

Black-necked Stilt It is a summer resident and breeder in the wetland.

American Avocet It is also a summer resident and breeds in the wetland.

Wilson's Phalarope It uses the wetland when moving through during both spring and fall migrations.

Great Horned Owl At least one owl has nested in one of the cottonwood trees. The best time to look is in the early spring before the trees have fully leafed out.

Willow Flycatcher The "Southwestern" *Empidonax* subspecies, federally desig-nated as endangered, is an uncommon summer resident and often breeds in the cottonwood bosque just beyond the western edge of the wildlife area.

American Pipit It is a winter resident. Look for it, fall through spring, in the plowed fields and along the edges of the wetlands and pond.

Red-winged and Yellow-headed Blackbirds Both species of blackbird are year-round residents and breeders, although the Red-winged Blackbird is much more prevalent. The easiest time to see one is during breeding season when the male protects its territory. During other times of the year, it leaves the wetland during the day to feed in nearby fields, returning at dusk in large mixed flocks.

Year-round residents include Canada Goose, Mallard, Ruddy Duck, Great Blue Heron, Red-tailed Hawk (more prevalent during winter), Cooper's Hawk, American Kestrel, American Coot, Killdeer, Mourning Dove, Greater Roadrunner, Northern Flicker, Black and Say's Phoebes, Loggerhead Shrike, American Crow (widespread during winter), Chihuahuan and Common Ravens, American Robin, European Starling, Great-tailed Grackle, House Finch, and Lesser Goldfinch.

Birds that winter at the wildlife area include Gadwall; American Wigeon; Northern Shoveler; Green-winged Teal; Northern Harrier; Ring-billed Gull (occasional); Savannah, Song, and White-crowned Sparrows; and Dark-eyed Junco.

Summer residents and breeders include Blue-winged and Cinnamon Teal, Snowy and Cattle Egrets, Green Heron, Spotted Sandpiper, and Black-chinned Hummingbird. Summer residents that nest in the vicinity and are fairly easy to spot, especially along the rear of the property closest to the bosque, include Western Wood-Pewee, Ash-throated Flycatcher, Western Kingbird, Common Yellowthroat, Yellow-breasted Chat, Summer Tanager, Blue Grosbeak, and Bullock's Oriole. Other summer visitors are Great Egret, Turkey Vulture, Swainson's Hawk, Common Nighthawk, and Barn Swallow.

The wildlife conservation area plays an important role in migration. Shorebirds regularly stopping over here include Solitary Sandpiper (fall only), Greater Yellowlegs, Western and Least Sandpipers, and Long-billed Dowitcher. Both Broad-tailed and Rufous Hummingbirds visit during fall migration. Passerines that migrate through the area include Plumbeous and Warbling Vireos; Tree, Violet-green, Northern Rough-winged, Bank, and Cliff Swallows; Blue-gray Gnatcatcher; Orange-crowned, Virginia's, Yellow, Yellow-rumped, and Wilson's Warblers; Green-tailed Towhee; and Chipping, Clay-colored, Brewer's, Vesper, and Lark Sparrows.

DIRECTIONS

By car: From the intersection of I-25 and I-40 in Albuquerque, take I-25 south approximately 30.5 miles to Exit 195 (I-25 Belen Business Bypass). Turn left and drive east on I-25 Bypass for 2.2 miles (this route passes near Belen Marsh; see site description). Merge right onto North Main Street (NM 314 W), and travel south for 2 miles. Turn left onto Reinken Avenue (NM 309 E), and travel east for approximately 2.4 miles. At about the halfway point, Reinken Road will merge with and become River Road (NM 309 E). After crossing the Rio Grande, turn left at Rio Communities Boulevard (NM 47). Whitfield Wildlife Conservation Area will be 1 mile north on the left.

Public transportation: None available

PARKING

There is a large parking area.

FEES

None

SPECIAL CONSIDERATIONS AND HAZARDS

- Rattlesnakes: Visitors should always be aware that rattlesnakes might be present during warm weather.
- Harvester ants: Before standing still to look at a bird, look down to make sure you are not standing on an anthill.
- Mosquitoes: They can be a problem at any place in the Rio Grande valley, but mostly in late summer and in the morning and evening hours.

FACILITIES

- Accessibility: There is wheelchair-accessible parking next to the Visitor Center. The roadway down to the wetlands is firm. If the gates leading from the parking lot to the conservation area are locked, special arrangements can be made to have them opened to provide access for wheelchairs (call in advance, 505-865-5807). The trail around the wildlife area is fairly level but often rutted and muddy following a storm.
- Restrooms: Restrooms are located in the Visitor Center.
- Water: There is a drinking fountain in the Visitor Center.
- Picnic tables: None available

FOOD, GAS, AND LODGING

Hotels are located off I-25 at Exit 191 (the next exit south of Exit 195 in the directions to the wildlife conservation area). Gas stations and restaurants are available along Main Street in Belen (see Whitfield WCA directions above).

Viewing platform on tour route

Bernardo Wildlife Management Area

DESCRIPTION

The Bernardo Wildlife Management Area, or Bernardo Unit of the Ladd S. Gordon Waterfowl Complex, is administered by the New Mexico Department of Game and Fish and is managed specifically to provide a winter habitat for waterfowl and Sandhill Cranes. While its 1,700 acres provide some of the best Sandhill Crane viewing in central New Mexico, it also attracts a variety of birds that make it an ideal year-round birding site.

After exiting I-25 and before entering the wildlife management area, begin your visit by driving east on U.S. 60 for about a mile. Make a U-turn, and pull off along the north side of the road to view the various seasonal ponds where often there are many wintering ducks and geese. Return west to NM 116, and turn right. Drive 1.7 miles north to the entrance of the wildlife management area.

During spring and summer, pause just beyond the entrance to inspect the fields and trees for passerines. In the winter, search the bare branches for raptors. Then proceed straight ahead on the auto tour route. Stop at the irrigation ditch, particularly during spring and fall migrations, as there will be a variety of swallows swooping over the water, and then continue to the first viewing platform. During the late fall and winter, climb the stairs to the platform, where you will gain a fairly close-up view of foraging Sandhill Cranes. Just to the north of this viewing area is a dirt road that provides access for refuge workers to reach the fields. In spring and summer and during fall migration, scan the bushes between the parking area and the road, as well as to the north of the road. Check the fields, which also attract different seasonal birds. Scour the trees west of the irrigation ditch and the foliage beside it. Next, drive south along the auto tour route and stop at the next viewing platform, which is accessed by a long ramp. Stop on the boardwalk as you walk over the irrigation ditch, and investigate the shrubs on either side. There may be some waterfowl in the ditch. The viewing platform provides opportunities to see both Sandhill Cranes and three species of geese during the late fall and winter.

As you drive along the auto tour route toward the final observation area, peruse the trees and fields for seasonal birds, and then stop at the parking area. There are two paths leading to observation blinds. Before continuing along the route, walk a short distance along the road (do not do this when Sandhill Cranes are on the road), inspecting the brush piles and branches of the cottonwood trees. A Great Horned Owl regularly nests in this area. Drive slowly along the remainder of the auto tour route, checking out the fields along the way.

The Bernardo Wildlife Management Area tour loop is open from one-half hour before sunrise until sunset from September 1 through March 9, and from 7:00 A.M. to sunset during the remainder of the year. The wildlife area occasionally is closed during hunting seasons or if wet weather causes the tour road to be too muddy. It is advisable to call before your visit for current information: 505-864-9187 or 505-476-8161.

County: Socorro

eBird Hotspot: Bernardo WMA

Web site for more information and map: www.wildlife.state.nm.us/conservation/wildlife_management_areas/documents/2007bernardo.pdf

Sandhill Crane Several thousand Sandhill Cranes winter at this location. The cranes often spend the day foraging in the fields and are easily observed from the viewing platforms and the auto tour route. During the late afternoon, they begin to make their way over to the seasonal ponds to provide safety from predators while they sleep. The cranes start arriving in mid-October and are gone by mid-March. The greatest numbers occur between late November and mid-February. In the late winter, you may often encounter cranes performing a series of leaps, hops, skips, and bows. Be sure to look for their large footprints, which may be visible along the road.

Snow Goose While a few Ross's Geese winter at this location, the greatest preponderance of light geese are Snow Geese. They arrive by mid-November and are gone by the end of February. Look for these geese foraging in the fields.

Say's Phoebe It often is perched on the tops of small twigs or on fence wires year-round.

Chihuahuan Raven While Common Raven also is reported here, this is a reliable location to see the Chihuahuan Raven. It is more prevalent during the winter months. Familiarize yourself with its call before your visit to assist with identification.

Marsh Wren It can be heard, and often seen, in the foliage along the irrigation ditches from October through April.

American Pipit It is present from mid-October through the end of March in freshly plowed fields. It often blends in and may look like a dirt clod until it moves.

Lark Sparrow It is plentiful in the fields from May through August.

OTHER BIRDS

Year-round birds include American Kestrel, Killdeer, Mourning and Eurasian Collared-Doves, Greater Roadrunner, Black Phoebe, Bewick's Wren, American Robin, Northern Mockingbird, Spotted Towhee, Red-winged Blackbird, Western Meadowlark, and House Finch. Some years a Great Horned Owl nests and roosts in one of the large cottonwood trees near the final viewing area.

Summer residents and nesters include Black-chinned Hummingbird, Western Wood-Pewee, Ash-throated Flycatcher, Western Kingbird, Cliff and Barn Swallows, Common Yellowthroat, Yellow-breasted Chat, Black-headed and Blue Grosbeaks, and Lesser Goldfinch.

Winter residents include Canada Goose, Cinnamon Teal (primarily March), Northern Shoveler, Northern Pintail, Green-winged Teal, Bald Eagle, Northern Harrier, Red-tailed Hawk, Wilson's Snipe, Northern Flicker, American Crow, Ruby-crowned Kinglet, Yellow-rumped Warbler, Song and White-crowned Sparrows, and Dark-eyed Junco.

During spring and fall migration, look for Gray Flycatcher, Wilson's Warbler, Western Tanager, Chipping Sparrow, and American Goldfinch.

DIRECTIONS

By car: From the intersection of I-25 and I-40 in Albuquerque, drive south on I-25 approximately 51 miles to Exit 175, Bernardo-Mountainair (U.S. 60 E). The cloverleaf ramp loops around under I-25, where you will be traveling east on U.S. 60. Continue east on U.S. 60 to view wintering waterfowl in the seasonal ponds as mentioned in the site description. Turn north on NM 116 at the intersection just east of the I-25 overpass to access the tour route. The wildlife area entrance will be on your right 1.7 miles north of U.S. 60.

Public transportation: None available

PARKING

There is ample parking at each of the viewing areas.

FEES

None. You may contribute to maintenance and habitat improvement projects at Bernardo and other wildlife management areas by purchasing a Gaining Access into Nature (GAIN) permit, a Habitat Stamp, or a Habitat Management and Access Validation, all available at New Mexico Fish and Game Department offices, online at www.wildlife.state.nm.us, or anywhere hunting and fishing licenses are sold in New Mexico.

SPECIAL CONSIDERATIONS AND HAZARDS

- Trash: Since there are no trash cans along the tour route, please pack out your trash.
- Hours: It is advisable to call New Mexico Fish and Game (505-864-9187 or 505-476-8161) to check whether the wildlife area is open and its hours, since these may vary from posted times.

- Accessibility: The second viewing platform has a wheelchair-accessible ramp. The trails at the last viewing area have a compacted surface to make them wheelchair accessible.
- Restrooms: Restrooms are available at the first and last viewing areas, and all are wheelchair accessible.
- Water: None available
- Picnic tables: There are a few picnic tables at the last viewing area, all of which are wheelchair accessible.

FOOD, GAS, AND LODGING

All services are available 15 miles north on I-25 at Exit 190, Belen, or 25 miles south on I-25 at Exit 190, Socorro.

Bosque del Apache National Wildlife Refuge

DESCRIPTION

Bosque del Apache is most famous for its wintering Sandhill Cranes and Snow Geese; however, it is often referred to as a "refuge for all seasons," with over 300 species. Fall is the beginning of a new cycle at the refuge. On October 1, the irrigation gates open to allow water to begin filling the ponds and marshes. Within 24 hours, many of the ponds have enough water to enable ducks to swim. Along with the water, the first of the wintering birds begin showing up. By mid-October, the early-bird Sandhill Cranes start arriving. The winter season kicks off with the Festival of the Cranes, held each year during the week before Thanksgiving. Among many other activities, the festival offers an opportunity for nature lovers with all levels of expertise to explore areas of the refuge normally not open to visitors and to learn from experts.

By late November approximately 18,000 cranes call the refuge their winter home—a thousand times the number that wintered here in 1940 before restoration efforts began. In addition, approximately 50,000 Snow Geese and 40,000–50,000 ducks spend the winter months on the refuge.

A spectacular treat while visiting the refuge in winter is to witness a morning fly-out. It can be worth shivering on a frosty deck to see the geese rise en masse against an orange sky. The cranes begin their clucking and morning conversations, and then they, too, leave in groups to head to nearby fields to feed.

By March, refuge personnel allow the water to begin draining from the seasonal ponds. The water levels recede in time for spring shorebird migration. The refuge is one of their major refueling stops. The first to arrive are large waders, followed in April by smaller shorebirds. By May, migration of flycatchers and other songbirds is in full swing, and species that nest at the refuge are setting up their territories. In spring and summer, hummingbirds buzz around the feeders outside the Visitor Center, and nesting birds are busy feeding their chicks. The seasonal road through the Farm Loop provides unique opportunities to view a variety of habitats.

Since it is at the northernmost range for a number of neotropical species, the refuge offers the possibility to view many species not normally seen in central New Mexico.

Begin your search for birds as you drive south from the village of San Antonio toward the refuge. Depending upon the time of year, a variety of birds that might not be present in the refuge itself can be viewed on the power lines, in the bushes along the road, and in the fields. The first seasonal ponds are along NM 1 just inside the refuge boundaries. These ponds are shorebird habitat during spring migration and often a prime location to view wintering geese and cranes at dusk.

Stop first at the Visitor Center where you can pick up a map of the refuge, take in various exhibits, peruse items in the nature shop, read the sightings logbook, ask questions of helpful volunteers, and watch birds through the observation window. During the summer months, visit the hummingbird feeders on the west side of the building. You can also purchase a CD that describes natural and historical highlights at various numbered stops along the audio tour route.

Before heading over to the tour route, take time to inspect the bushes and trees that border the parking lot. Walk around the perimeter of the pavilion area and through the Desert Arboretum, checking for birds that visit the feeders at the employee residences beyond. As you exit the parking lot, pull over on the left-hand side of the road to view the permanent wetlands bordering NM 1.

When you enter the tour loop area, start your visit on the Marsh Loop, a 7-mile section of the road that has both seasonal and year-round ponds managed for waterfowl. Stop at each observation deck, and scan the ponds and foliage along the road. Each seasonal pond seems to attract a different set of species, so it is worth a look at each one.

Birders on boardwalk

At audio tour stop 3 (marked with a sign), walk out on a boardwalk over one of the permanent wetlands. As you continue along the tour route, a year-round pond with dead trees will be on your left where the Marsh Loop joins the two-way road (audio tour stop 10). This area is a Black-crowned Night-Heron rookery. When you get to the two-way road, turn left (consult map available at Visitor Center) and drive until you reach the observation deck on your right, the Eagle Scout Deck. This is an excellent vantage point at all times of the year.

Next, continue on the tour route by backtracking on the two-way road to the Farm Loop, which heads to the left (and is open year-round) or by taking the seasonal road that heads to the left (north) beside the Eagle Scout Deck (April 1–September 30).

The Farm Loop, a 7.5-mile road, passes three observation decks (Chupadera, Willow, and Coyote—the seasonal road bypasses these). The decks overlook the fields where cranes and geese feed in the winter during the late afternoon. Bare snags, favored by wintering raptors, surround the fields. As you round the north end of the Farm Loop, stop to gaze down the refuge maintenance road. Several large cottonwood trees often serve as perching spots for birds during the winter. The Farm Deck and other turnouts provide ample opportunities to watch Snow Geese and Sandhill Cranes as they feed frenetically in the late afternoon. You may witness the drama between the geese and coyotes as the coyotes try to sneak unseen by the geese along the concrete ditches between the fields. You might even glimpse a pile of white feathers representing a coyote's or eagle's lunch leftovers. When the cranes and geese are finished feeding, they rise up and fly farther into the refuge in large groups.

The Phil Norton Observation Blind provides peeping holes into permanent wetlands and is worth a look at any time of the year.

Just past audio tour stop 14 is the Flight Deck. In the winter you will want to arrive as dusk approaches. The deck can be crowded with birders, photographers, and other visitors. As the sun slips over Chupadera Peak, the Sandhill Cranes began to fly into the safety of the shallow water to spend the night. The Flight Deck is also the prime location to experience the fly-out of cranes and geese early in the morning, just as the first of the sun's rays begin peeking over the distant mountains.

Often overlooked parts of the refuge are the Chupadera and Canyon Loop Trails. The Chupadera Wilderness Trail leading to Chupadera Peak, an ascent of 1,700 feet, is a 9.5-mile round-trip. However, walking only a mile or two along the trail will provide opportunities to see birds that frequent the Chihuahuan desert scrub habitat. The trailhead for the Chupadera Trail is north of the Visitor Center on NM 1. The Canyon Loop Nature Trail traverses a 2.5-mile circular route through Solitude Canyon, also a Chihuahuan desert scrub habitat. The trailhead is 1.6 miles south of the Visitor Center on NM 1.

The tour loop and nature trails are open every day of the year from one hour before sunrise to one hour after sunset. The Visitor Center is open from 7:30 A.M. to 4:00 P.M. on weekdays and 8:00 A.M. to 4:30 P.M. on Saturdays and Sundays. The Visitor Center is closed on Christmas Day, New Year's Day, and the Fourth of July.

County: Socorro

eBird Hotspots: Bosque del Apache NWR (For those wanting more specificity, there are separate eBird Hotspots for Marsh Loop, Farm Loop, Seasonal Road, Hwy 1 to north—Observation Area, and Visitor Center.)

Web site for more information: www.friendsofthebosque.org/Friends index.html

TARGET BIRDS

Snow and Ross's Geese Approximately 50,000 Snow Geese and several hundred Ross's Geese make the refuge their winter home. Both species flock and roost together. By scanning the flocks carefully, you can pick out the slightly smaller Ross's Geese with their plain bills. Look for both species as they forage in the cornfields or from the Flight or Eagle Scout Decks at dusk or dawn. Snow Geese begin arriving in mid-October and are present at the refuge in substantial numbers through the end of February. Ross's Geese generally arrive at the end of October or early November and are also gone by the end of February.

Ring-necked Pheasant The white-winged race of this species at the Bosque del Apache has a barely visible neck ring. It often can be glimpsed scurrying across the road.

Wild Turkey While it is a year-round resident, it is not usually seen until the ponds are drained in spring. It most often is encountered in small groups on the seasonal road during the summer months.

American White Pelican The refuge is on the migration route of the American White Pelican. During both spring and fall migrations it can be seen flying overhead in large flocks and often is seen on the permanent pond near the boardwalk. The break in the foliage at audio tour stop 1 is often a good place to spot it.

Neotropic and Double-crested Cormorants Both are year-round residents at the refuge. The Neotropic Cormorant normally frequents the pond along NM 1 across from the Visitor Center, the pond by the boardwalk, and the rookery pond at audio tour stop 10. The less prevalent Double-crested Cormorant is often interspersed with the Neotropic.

Great Blue Heron You are sure to spot at least two or three Great Blue Herons in the drainage ditches as you follow the tour route.

Black-crowned Night-Heron It is a year-round resident; however, it is seen most easily during spring at the rookery (audio tour stop 10) when it gathers with others to nest. At other times of the year, it is more spread out and is a solitary hunter.

Bald Eagle Adult and immature Bald Eagles winter at the refuge. They can be seen perched on snags. The best location to view one is from the Eagle Scout or Flight Deck during December and January.

Sandhill Crane It begins arriving at Bosque del Apache in late October, and by the end of November approximately 18,000 cranes have settled in for the winter. They begin leaving at the end of February.

Greater Roadrunner You will probably see at least one prancing along the road as you loop through the refuge.

Lesser and Common Nighthawks Both Lesser and Common Nighthawks nest at the refuge. They are present from May through early September; however, both of their numbers are highest during May when there is still some water in the seasonal ponds.

Vermilion Flycatcher The refuge is at the northern edge of its range. While the Vermilion Flycatcher is not always seen during the summer months, a few are usually present. Occasionally, one has been spotted during the winter.

Sandhill Cranes (Photo by Bonnie L. Long)

Chihuahuan Raven Both Common and Chihuahuan Ravens are seen at the refuge, but the most prevalent is the Chihuahuan Raven. Although its call is hoarse-sounding, it is slightly higher-pitched than the call of a Common Raven, and the base of its neck feathers are white rather than gray. Ravens have nested under the railroad trestle south of the Visitor Center on NM 1.

Verdin It is a year-round resident and nests at the refuge. It is frequently seen flitting in the foliage bordering the Visitor Center parking lot.

American Pipit It has been reported at various locations from October through May. The pipit scavenges for insects after the refuge staff plows under the summer cover crops and before water is let into the seasonal ponds. During winter months, look for dirt clods that seem to move in the fields along NM-1 between San Antonio and the refuge. Again in the spring, find it in freshly tilled fields in both locations. It is often in mixed flocks with Horned Larks and very occasionally with Chestnut-collared Longspurs.

Pyrrhuloxia It is a year-round resident and breeder and often is glimpsed in the grass and scrub just behind the pavilion.

Lucy's Warbler The refuge is at the northern edge of its range. Listen and watch for it in the cottonwood trees along the seasonal road when it arrives in early April.

Phainopepla It is present in the spring and summer and nests at the refuge. It can be seen most often in the spring in the trees near the Visitor Center.

American Goldfinch The refuge is one of the wintering grounds for the American Goldfinch. The refuge also is a stopover during fall migration for individuals heading farther south. It feeds on stands of dried wild sunflowers.

OTHER BIRDS

Winter: A large variety of waterfowl spend the winter at the refuge. There is a large population of Canada Geese, along with smaller numbers of Cackling Geese. Look for the Cackling Geese in the seasonal pond on the south end of the Marsh Loop. Ducks that winter at the refuge and almost always can be seen include Gadwall, American Wigeon, Northern Shoveler, Northern Pintail, Green-winged Teal, Canvasback, Redhead, Ring-necked Duck, Bufflehead, and Hooded and Common Mergansers. The refuge is also a wintering home for several raptors, the most prevalent being Red-tailed Hawk, Northern Harrier, and American Kestrel. In addition, you might spot a Ferruginous Hawk, Golden Eagle, or Prairie Falcon. The edges of the irrigation ditches in the winter may harbor Greater Yellowlegs, Killdeer, and

Wilson's Snipe. Check large nestlike silhouettes in taller cottonwoods along the Marsh Loop for napping porcupines. As you drive south from San Antonio, keep your eyes peeled for Loggerhead Shrike. From October through April, listen for Marsh Wren in the reeds near the various observation decks. Several sparrows winter at the refuge, including Song and White-crowned (occasionally with a White-throated mixed in), and Dark-eyed Junco. Yellow-rumped Warblers and Ruby-crowned Kinglets can be present near the observation decks on the Farm Loop. Yellow-headed and Brewer's Blackbirds often are perched in mixed flocks in bare trees on the Farm Loop. Sage Sparrow may be found along either the Chupadera or Canyon Loop Trail.

During migration: As cranes, waterfowl, and the wintering birds head north, other birds begin arriving. The refuge plays an important role in both spring and fall migrations, but spring is a particularly active time. White-faced Ibis, American Avocet, Black-necked Stilt, and Great Egret probe the shallow water in the seasonal ponds near the Flight Deck, at the beginning of the seasonal road, and near audio tour stop 3. In both spring and fall look for Sora; Western, Least, and Baird's Sandpipers, as well as less prevalent sandpipers; Long-billed Dowitcher; Wilson's Phalarope (primarily spring); Ring-billed Gull; and Black Tern (some years). Tree and Violet-green Swallows swoop over the seasonal ponds as they migrate through. Western Tanagers and a variety of sparrows can be seen at this time. Although they are year-round residents, Red-winged Blackbirds are most spectacular during the spring. Look for Lesser Goldfinch gorging on sunflower seeds on the Farm Loop in the fall.

Summer: While the refuge is known for its wintering waterfowl, it is also the summer home for Blue-winged and Cinnamon Teal. Summer raptors include Turkey Vulture and Swainson's Hawk. A number of species are summer residents and breeders in the lush bosque. Snowy and Cattle Egrets, Green Heron, and Spotted Sandpiper nest in the refuge and can be found along some of the irrigation ditches. You may see a variety of summer flycatchers, including Western Wood-Pewee, Ash-throated Flycatcher, and Western Kingbird. Four species of swallows nest at the refuge—Northern Rough-winged, Bank, Cliff, and Barn. Listen and look for Common Yellowthroat and Yellow-breasted Chat in the willows. You will easily spot brightly colored Summer Tanager and Blue and Black-headed Grosbeaks in cottonwood trees along the inside of the Marsh Loop. You can often catch a glimpse of a Bullock's Oriole near the Visitor Center. Check the fields for Lark Sparrow.

Year-round: Many species are permanent residents at the refuge. Canada Goose, Mallard, and Ruddy Duck are in the ponds at any time of the year, along with Pied-billed, Western, and Clark's Grebes and American Coot. Gambel's Quail is most easily seen near the Visitor Center in the spring when the male might be perched to protect its territory and in June when you might be lucky enough to see a covey of chicks. Watch for a flash of red wings as the Northern Flicker flies between trees or is ground-feeding on the Farm Loop. Black Phoebe surveys the irrigation ditches and ponds on overhanging bushes. Say's Phoebe can be seen perched on low stalks almost anywhere in the refuge and often nests near the Visitor Center. Loggerhead Shrike is most easily spotted during fall and winter on power lines along NM-1 or when you tour the Farm Loop. Bewick's Wren can be found at any time of the year in dense shrubs. Listen for its melodic song in the spring when the male is on its nesting territory. Watch for Western Meadowlarks in the grasses along the tour routes and Black-throated Sparrow, Northern Mockingbird, Curve-billed and Crissal Thrashers, and Rock Wren in desert scrub habitat.

DIRECTIONS

By car: From the intersection of I-40 and I-25 in Albuquerque, travel south on I-25 for approximately 87 miles to Exit 139, San Antonio–Carrizozo (U.S. 370). Drive east approximately 2 miles on U.S. 370 to San Antonio. At the flashing light, turn right (south) onto Main Street (NM 1) and drive approximately 8 miles. Bosque del Apache Visitor Center will be on the right.

Public transportation: None available

PARKING

There is a large parking lot at the Visitor Center and parking areas adjacent to all observation decks.

FEES

A $3.00 fee per vehicle is payable at the Tour Loop entrance station. (If the station is unattended, put your fee in the envelope and drop it in the slot.) There is no fee required for visitors with a federal access pass or current Federal Duck Stamp.

■ Rattlesnakes: Watch and listen for rattlesnakes during warm weather, especially during the evening. Five species of rattlesnakes live on the refuge and have been seen near the residences, as well as in less developed areas.

■ Mosquitoes: You might encounter mosquitoes on the observation decks, along trails, and at the pavilion picnic area from spring through early fall.

■ Yellow jackets and bees: Be alert for stinging insects nesting under the boardwalks and decks, particularly in late summer.

FACILITIES

■ Accessibility: All restrooms and observation decks are wheelchair accessible.

■ Restrooms: Restrooms are available at the Visitor Center and at several locations along the tour route.

■ Water: There is a drinking fountain in the Visitor Center.

■ Picnic tables: There are covered picnic tables in the pavilion near the Desert Arboretum at the Visitor Center.

FOOD, GAS, AND LODGING

A gas station; restaurants, including the historic Owl Bar and Café (closed Sunday); and bed-and-breakfast-style lodging are available in the village of San Antonio 8 miles north of the refuge at or near the intersection of NM 1 and U.S. 380. There is an RV campground just north of the refuge on NM 1. The nearest hotels (and more restaurants and gas stations) are in the town of Socorro, approximately 8 miles north of San Antonio on I-25 (or NM 1).

CHAPTER 9

American Birding Association's Code of Birding Ethics

Everyone who enjoys birds and birding must always respect wildlife, its environment, and the rights of others. In any conflict of interest between birds and birders, the welfare of the birds and their environment comes first. The Code of Birding Ethics developed by ABA is available on the ABA Web site: www.aba.org.

Code of Birding Ethics

1. Promote the welfare of birds and their environment.
1(a) Support the protection of important bird habitat.
1(b) To avoid stressing birds or exposing them to danger, exercise restraint and caution during observation, photography, sound recording, or filming.

Limit the use of recordings and other methods of attracting birds, and never use such methods in heavily birded areas or for attracting any species that is Threatened, Endangered, or of Special Concern, or is rare in your local area.

Keep well back from nests and nesting colonies, roosts, display areas, and important feeding sites. In such sensitive areas, if there is a need for extended observation, photography, filming, or recording, try to use a blind or hide and take advantage of natural cover.

Use artificial light sparingly for filming or photography, especially for close-ups.

1(c) Before advertising the presence of a rare bird, evaluate the potential for disturbance to the bird, its surroundings, and other people in the area, and proceed only if access can be controlled, disturbance minimized, and permission has been obtained from private landowners. The sites of rare nesting birds should be divulged only to the proper conservation authorities.

1(d) Stay on roads, trails, and paths where they exist; otherwise, keep habitat disturbance to a minimum.

2. Respect the law, and the rights of others.

2(a) Do not enter private property without the owner's explicit permission.

2(b) Follow all laws, rules, and regulations governing use of roads and public areas, both at home and abroad.

2(c) Practice common courtesy in contacts with other people. Your exemplary behavior will generate goodwill with birders and nonbirders alike.

3. Ensure that feeders, nest structures, and other artificial bird environments are safe.

3(a) Keep dispensers, water, and food clean and free of decay or disease. It is important to feed birds continually during harsh weather.

3(b) Maintain and clean nest structures regularly.

3(c) If you are attracting birds to an area, ensure the birds are not exposed to predation from cats and other domestic animals or dangers posed by artificial hazards.

4. Group birding, whether organized or impromptu, requires special care.

Each individual in the group, in addition to the obligations spelled out in Items #1 and #2, has responsibilities as a Group Member.

4(a) Respect the interests, rights, and skills of fellow birders, as well as people participating in other legitimate outdoor activities. Freely share your knowledge and experience, except where code 1(c) applies. Be especially helpful to beginning birders.

4(b) If you witness unethical birding behavior, assess the situation and intervene if you think it prudent. When interceding, inform the person(s) of the inappropriate action and attempt, within reason, to have it stopped. If the behavior continues, document it, and notify appropriate individuals or organizations.

Group Leader Responsibilities (amateur and professional trips and tours).

4(c) Be an exemplary ethical role model for the group. Teach through word and example.

4(d) Keep groups to a size that limits impact on the environment and does not interfere with others using the same area.

4(e) Ensure everyone in the group knows of and practices this code.

4(f) Learn and inform the group of any special circumstances applicable to the areas being visited (e.g., no tape recorders allowed).

4(g) Acknowledge that professional tour companies bear a special responsibility to place the welfare of birds and the benefits of public knowledge ahead of the company's commercial interests. Ideally, leaders should keep track of tour sightings, document unusual occurrences, and submit records to appropriate organizations.

Please follow this Code and distribute and teach it to others.

Annotated Checklist

Most of the 241 species listed here are those mentioned in one or more of the site descriptions. Also included are species that are seen regularly in central New Mexico but not with regularity at any of the sites. Species documented in central New Mexico but considered rarities or vagrants are not included. Report any species not included on the follwing list to the New Mexico Bird Records Committee (see "Local Birding Information and Resources" in chapter 2).

The following abbreviations are used:

- NM: National Monument
- NWR: National Wildlife Refuge
- Quarai: Salinas National Monument–Quarai Site
- RGNC: Rio Grande Nature Center
- WCA: Wildlife Conservation Area
- WMA: Wildlife Management Area

The sequence and names conform to the American Ornithologists' Union's *Check-list of North American Birds*, 7th ed. (1998) as amended through its 51st Supplement (July 2010). These abundance terms are used in this checklist:

- Abundant: Referring to a species that is numerous
- Common: Likely to be seen or heard in suitable habitat
- Uncommon: Present, but not certain to be seen
- Occasional: Seen only a few times during a season

Greater White-fronted Goose (*Anser albifrons*): Occasional during winter at Bosque del Apache NWR and RGNC.

Snow Goose (*Chen caerulescens*): Abundant during winter, primarily at the Bosque del Apache NWR, although sometimes spotted foraging in agricultural fields. Arrives in mid-October and can be seen in abundance through the end of February, although stragglers may remain as late as early April.

Ross's Goose (*Chen rossii*): Can be found mingling with the flocks of Snow Geese at Bosque del Apache NWR. Generally does not arrive until the end of October or early November and is gone by the end of February.

Cackling Goose (*Branta hutchinsii*): A large flock winters on the middle Rio Grande, arriving in late October or early November and remaining until mid-March. The easiest place to observe this species is mid- to late morning in the parking-lot pond at the RGNC.

Canada Goose (*Branta canadensis*): Common year-round resident, and by mid-October becomes abundant as wintering flocks arrive, remaining until mid-March. Can be seen foraging in agricultural fields, on the river, or at Bosque del Apache NWR, Bernardo WMA, or RGNC.

Wood Duck (*Aix sponsa*): A year-round resident; abundant in the main pond at the RGNC or at Alameda Open Space wetlands.

Gadwall (*Anas strepera*): A common winter resident arriving in early October and often lingering through early May. The best places to see this species are the Alameda Open Space, RGNC, and Bosque del Apache NWR.

American Wigeon (*Anas americana*): A common winter resident that can be observed at the Bosque del Apache NWR, the RGNC's parking-lot pond, Alameda Open Space, on the river from the Corrales Bosque, and occasionally during migration at the Belen Marsh and Whitfield WCA.

Mallard (*Anas platyrhynchos*): An abundant year-round resident found almost anywhere there is water.

Blue-winged Teal (*Anas discors*): An uncommon summer resident and breeder, arriving as early as April and present through October. It is possible to spot it at the RGNC, Belen Marsh, Whitfield WCA, and Bosque del Apache NWR.

Cinnamon Teal (*Anas cyanoptera*): A common summer resident and breeder and uncommon throughout the winter. Look for it at the Belen Marsh, Whitfield WCA, Bernardo WMA, and Bosque del Apache NWR and occasionally in the parking-lot pond at the RGNC.

Northern Shoveler (*Anas clypeata*): A common to abundant winter resident and uncommon throughout the summer. Look for it at sites with year-round and seasonal ponds, as well as on the Rio Grande.

Northern Pintail (*Anas acuta*): It is common at the Bosque del Apache NWR, which is an important wintering site for this species. Uncommon at other sites along middle Rio Grande. Arrives mid-October, with the numbers peaking in December, and also winters at Bernardo WMA.

Green-winged Teal (*Anas crecca*): Common during the winter at the RGNC, Belen Marsh, Whitfield WCA, and Bernardo WMA. The largest numbers are at the Bosque del Apache NWR.

Canvasback (*Aythya valisineria*): Uncommon in winter. The best chance to see one is at the Bosque del Apache NWR.

Redhead (*Aythya americana*): Uncommon in winter. The best chance to see one is at the Bosque del Apache NWR.

Ring-necked Duck (*Aythya collaris*): Among the earliest wintering ducks to arrive. The best place to spot one, from early October until April, is on the observation pond at the RGNC. It can also be seen at Alameda Open Space wetlands and Bosque del Apache NWR.

Lesser Scaup (*Aythya affinis*): An uncommon winter resident occasionally seen at the RGNC; however, it is more prevalent at the Bosque del Apache NWR.

Bufflehead (*Bucephala albeola*): Uncommon during the winter at the Bosque del Apache NWR and occasional at the RGNC.

Hooded Merganser (*Lophodytes cucullatus*): Uncommon; one or two usually are present during the winter at the RGNC, as well at the Bosque del Apache NWR.

Common Merganser (*Mergus merganser*): Common on the river at Alameda Open Space, Corrales Bosque, and the Bosque del Apache NWR.

Ruddy Duck (*Oxyura jamaicensis*): Common to uncommon year-round at the RGNC, Belen Marsh, Whitfield WCA, and the Bosque del Apache NWR.

Scaled Quail (*Callipepla squamata*): Native to central New Mexico's scrub habitat and common year-round in the Sandia Foothills and Petroglyph NM. The easiest time to spot one is during breeding season.

Gambel's Quail (*Callipepla gambelii*): Native to the desert southwest north to Albuquerque, it now is found at higher altitudes, including the Sandia Foothills and Petroglyph NM. Common year-round at the Bosque del Apache NWR.

Ring-necked Pheasant (*Phasianus colchicus*): A common year-round resident in the agricultural fields adjacent to the RGNC. The white-winged race (*P. c. chrysomelas*) is seen at the Bosque del Apache NWR.

Wild Turkey (*Meleagris gallopavo*): Uncommon year-round. The best time to spot one at the Bosque del Apache NWR is during the summer on the seasonal road; it can also be spotted on the trails in the Sandia Mountains or in Tajique Canyon in the Manzano Mountains.

Pied-billed Grebe (*Podilymbus podiceps*): Common year-round on lakes and ponds. Search for one at the RGNC and the Bosque del Apache NWR.

Western Grebe (*Aechmophorus occidentalis*): Uncommon in the deep-water boardwalk pond at the Bosque del Apache NWR, spring through fall.

Clark's Grebe (*Aechmophorus clarkii*): An occasional resident found during the summer in the deep-water boardwalk pond at the Bosque del Apache NWR.

Neotropic Cormorant (*Phalacrocorax brasilianus*): Occasional north of the Bosque del Apache NWR, which is its normal northernmost range in New Mexico. Uncommon at the refuge, it often perches in the permanent wetlands near the entrance booth to the refuge tour route during wet years when there is sufficient water, as well as in the rookery pond.

Double-crested Cormorant (*Phalacrocorax auritus*): Seen occasionally, it has been less prevalent in recent years; often mixed with Neotropic Cormorants at the Bosque del Apache NWR.

American White Pelican (*Pelecanus erythrorhynchos*): Large flocks wing their way north and south through central New Mexico during migration. Uncommon, it can be spotted flying overhead or resting in the boardwalk pond at the Bosque del Apache NWR.

Great Blue Heron (*Ardea herodias*): Abundant year-round at the Bosque del Apache NWR and common at Whitfield WCA or anywhere along the Rio Grande.

Great Egret (*Ardea alba*): An uncommon summer resident and breeder that often can be found at the Bosque del Apache NWR and sometimes at Whitfield WCA, as well as other places along the middle Rio Grande.

Snowy Egret (*Egretta thula*): Common summer resident and breeder that begins to arrive mid-March and lingers through October. It often can be seen at the RGNC, Alameda Open Space, Albuquerque Open Space Visitor Center, Los Lunas River Park, Belen Marsh (where it flies in to spend the night), Whitfield WCA, and the Bosque del Apache NWR.

Cattle Egret (*Bubulcus ibis*): An uncommon summer resident and breeder, arriving in March and lingering into November. During the day, it primarily forages in agricultural fields and flies to ponds for the night. The best places to see one are Los Lunas River Park, Whitfield WCA, the Bosque del Apache NWR, or an hour before dusk at the Belen Marsh.

Green Heron (*Butorides virescens*): An uncommon summer resident and migrant that might be spotted anywhere along the middle Rio Grande. Can be seen reliably at the RGNC, Whitfield WCA, and Bosque del Apache NWR.

Black-crowned Night-Heron (*Nycticorax nycticorax*): Primarily a common summer resident and migrant along the river and on ponds, but a few stay on through the winter. Look for one in the summer at the RGNC and Albuquerque Open Space Visitor Center, and year-round along the west bank of the river north of the old bridge at Alameda Open Space and at Bosque del Apache NWR.

Glossy Ibis (*Plegadis falcinellus*): Found occasionally during spring migration in flocks of White-faced Ibis.

White-faced Ibis (*Plegadis chihi*): A common spring (mid-March through May) and fall (mid-August through mid-October) migrant most frequently seen at Alameda Open Space, Belen Marsh, Whitfield WCA, and the Bosque del Apache NWR. Occasionally one or two are spotted during the winter.

Turkey Vulture (*Cathartes aura*): A common migrant and summer resident in all areas of central New Mexico.

Osprey (*Pandion haliaetus*): An uncommon migrant, primarily in spring from mid-March through May, often seen at the Sandia HawkWatch site (Three Gun Spring) and occasionally at the RGNC and Bosque del Apache NWR.

Mississippi Kite (*Ictinia mississippiensis*): An uncommon summer resident that breeds in the cottonwood bosque along the middle Rio Grande. It is most reliably seen at the Los Lunas River Park.

Bald Eagle (*Haliaeetus leucocephalus*): A common winter visitor along the middle Rio Grande, arriving at the beginning of November, reaching a peak during December and January, and gone by March. Check along the river at the Alameda Open Space and Corrales Bosque or on snags at Whitfield WCA, Bernardo WMA, and Bosque del Apache NWR.

Northern Harrier (*Circus cyaneus*): A common winter resident, arriving in mid-August and departing by mid-May. It courses over fields and marshes. Look for it at the RGNC, Albuquerque Open Space Visitor Center, Whitfield WCA, and Bosque del Apache NWR. It is also seen during migration at the Sandia HawkWatch site (Three Gun Spring).

Sharp-shinned Hawk (*Accipiter striatus*): An uncommon winter resident and migrant, arriving in early September and remaining until April, that prefers montane habitats at lower elevations. Search for it at the RGNC and other sites along the middle Rio Grande, south to the Bosque del Apache NWR. It is also one of the most frequently seen raptors at both HawkWatch sites (Three Gun and Capilla Peak) during migration.

Cooper's Hawk (*Accipiter cooperii*): A migrant as well as a common year-round resident and breeder found in abundance throughout central New Mexico.

Northern Goshawk (*Accipiter gentilis*): An occasional year-round resident of the Sandia Mountains that breeds below Balsam Glade overlook.

Broad-winged Hawk (*Buteo platypterus*): An occasional migrant through the Sandia and Manzano Mountains, primarily spotted at either the spring (Three Gun) or fall (Capilla Peak) HawkWatch site.

Swainson's Hawk (*Buteo swainsoni*): A common summer resident and breeder, primarily in open areas along the middle Rio Grande.

Red-tailed Hawk (*Buteo jamaicensis*): Widespread throughout central New Mexico. It may be an uncommon year-round resident, but it is much more common during the winter. It is possible to see one at any of the sites. Scan the tops of power poles along the interstates.

Ferruginous Hawk (*Buteo regalis*): An uncommon migrant and winter resident in grassland locations. The most reliable place to spot one is at the Bosque del Apache NWR.

Rough-legged Hawk (*Buteo lagopus*): Occasional during fall migration, primarily at the fall HawkWatch site at Capilla Peak.

Golden Eagle (*Aquila chrysaetos*): Occasional during winter, as well as a migrant. One or two usually winter at the Bosque del Apache NWR.

American Kestrel (*Falco sparverius*): A common year-round resident and breeder in open areas. Good places to observe one are the RGNC and Whitfield WCA, on power lines along NM 337 and NM 55, and on NM 1 south of San Antonio to the Bosque del Apache NWR.

Merlin (*Falco columbarius*): An uncommon migrant and winter resident. Besides at the HawkWatch sites, you might see one in the Sandia Foothills during migration and occasionally at Bernardo WMA and Bosque del Apache NWR during the winter.

Aplomado Falcon (*Falco femoralis*): Once common in grassland and open marsh habitat, it has been on the endangered species list since 1986.

Falcons of the "northern" subspecies (*F. c. septentrionalis*) released at Armendariz Ranch, as part of a recovery program, occasionally hunt at Bosque del Apache NWR.

Peregrine Falcon (*Falco peregrinus*): An occasional migrant most reliably seen at the HawkWatch sites. It occasionally nests on rocky ledges in remote areas of the Sandia and Manzano Mountains.

Prairie Falcon (*Falco mexicanus*): An occasional migrant and winter resident in open areas; seen regularly each winter at the Bosque del Apache NWR.

Virginia Rail (*Rallus limicola*): An occasional migrant that has been documented year-round at the Belen Marsh.

Sora (*Porzana carolina*): An occasional migrant spotted almost annually at the Belen Marsh.

Common Moorhen (*Gallinula chloropus*): An occasional visitor at Bosque del Apache NWR.

American Coot (*Fulica americana*): Abundant to common year-round resident in ponds and wetlands. It can be observed on the ponds at the RGNC, Alameda Open Space, Belen Marsh, Whitfield WCA, and Bosque del Apache NWR.

Sandhill Crane (*Grus canadensis*): Common to abundant during winter along the middle Rio Grande, with the largest population at the Bosque del Apache NWR. It begins to arrive in mid-October and has departed by the end of March. During the day, you might see it in fields near the RGNC, Albuquerque Open Space Visitor Center, Whitfield WCA, and Bernardo WMA or foraging at the Bosque del Apache NWR, but it often flies out into nearby fields, returning in large flocks to the refuge in the late afternoon, where the birds spend the night in one of the refuge ponds. Individuals wintering farther north spend the night in the Rio Grande.

Semipalmated Plover (*Charadrius semipalmatus*): Occasional migrant that might be spotted at Belen Marsh, Whitfield WCA, or Bosque del Apache NWR.

Killdeer (*Charadrius vociferus*): A common year-round resident and breeder near ponds and mudflats; easily spotted at the RGNC, Belen Marsh, Whitfield WCA, Bernardo WMA, and Bosque del Apache NWR.

Black-necked Stilt (*Himantopus mexicanus*): A spring migrant at the Bosque del Apache NWR and common summer resident and breeder at the Belen Marsh and Whitfield WCA.

American Avocet (*Recurvirostra americana*): A spring, and occasional fall, migrant at the Bosque del Apache NWR and summer resident and breeder at the Belen Marsh and Whitfield WCA.

Spotted Sandpiper (*Actitis macularius*): A locally common migrant and summer breeder. Look for it along the parking-lot pond at the RGNC, the edges of Manzano Pond, and in the Mountainair sewage ponds during migration, Belen Marsh, Whitfield WCA, and the Bosque del Apache NWR.

Solitary Sandpiper (*Tringa solitaria*): Seen occasionally during migration at the Belen Marsh, Whitfield WCA, and Bosque del Apache NWR, primarily in fall (mid-July through end of September).

Greater Yellowlegs (*Tringa melanoleuca*): An uncommon migrant in both spring and fall. The best opportunity to spot one is at the Belen Marsh, Whitfield WCA, and the Bosque del Apache NWR; an uncommon winter resident at the Bosque del Apache NWR.

Willet (*Tringa semipalmata*): An uncommon migrant mid-April through mid-May.

Lesser Yellowlegs (*Tringa flavipes*): An uncommon migrant in both spring and fall.

Western Sandpiper (*Calidris mauri*): A common migrant, April through mid-May and mid-July through September, at Belen Marsh, Whitfield WCA, and Bosque del Apache NWR.

Least Sandpiper (*Calidris minutilla*): A common migrant, March through mid-May and mid-July through September, at the Belen Marsh, Whitfield WCA, and Bosque del Apache NWR.

Baird's Sandpiper (*Calidris bairdii*): A common migrant, primarily mid-July through early October, at the Belen Marsh and Mountainair sewage ponds.

Pectoral Sandpiper (*Calidris melanotos*): An uncommon migrant, mid-August through early October, at the Belen Marsh and Mountainair sewage ponds.

Stilt Sandpiper (*Calidris himantopus*): An uncommon migrant, mid-July through September, at Belen Marsh and Bosque del Apache NWR.

Long-billed Dowitcher (*Limnodromus scolopaceus*): A common migrant in both spring and fall that often winters at the Bosque del Apache NWR. Search for it at the Belen Marsh, at Whitfield WCA, and in the seasonal wetlands along NM 1 at the Bosque del Apache NWR.

Wilson's Snipe (*Gallinago delicata*): An uncommon migrant and winter resident in marshes and along drainage ditches. Look for it at the RGNC, Alameda Open Space, Bernardo WMA, and Bosque del Apache NWR.

Wilson's Phalarope (*Phalaropus tricolor*): A common spring and fall migrant that can be seen regularly April and May and mid-July through mid-September at the Belen Marsh, Whitfield WCA, and Bosque del Apache NWR.

Red-necked Phalarope (*Phalaropus lobatus*): Occasional fall migrant, primarily at Bosque del Apache NWR.

Franklin's Gull (*Leucophaeus pipixcan*): An uncommon migrant seen regularly during April at the Belen Marsh and sometimes at Bosque del Apache NWR, along the middle Rio Grande, and at the RGNC.

Ring-billed Gull (*Larus delawarensis*): Although it might be spotted anywhere along the middle Rio Grande during the winter, it is common north of the Alameda Bridge and along the Corrales Bosque.

Black Tern (*Chlidonias niger*): An occasional spring and fall migrant, primarily at Bosque del Apache NWR.

Rock Pigeon (*Columba livia*): Abundant in urban areas.

Band-tailed Pigeon (*Patagioenas fasciata*): An uncommon summer resident in the Sandia and Manzano Mountains. Scan the tops of conifers along the Sandia Crest Highway. It is also a reliable visitor to the Capulin Spring log.

Eurasian Collared-Dove (*Streptopelia decaocto*): A common introduced species, now well established and widespread throughout central New Mexico.

White-winged Dove (*Zenaida asiatica*): An abundant year-round resident throughout central New Mexico.

Mourning Dove (*Zenaida macroura*): An abundant migrant and year-round resident, primarily in the middle Rio Grande valley, at lower elevations in the Sandia Mountains, along NM 337 and NM 55, and at Petroglyph NM. It moves from the mountains into the valleys during winter.

Inca Dove (*Columbina inca*): An uncommon year-round resident, not seen regularly at any particular spot. In central New Mexico, it is rarely seen sitting on power lines, preferring to perch in the branches of trees and forage in the grass. It is reported regularly in the neighborhoods near the University of New Mexico and in some areas of Albuquerque's northeast heights. It is also possible at the Bosque del Apache NWR.

Greater Roadrunner (*Geococcyx californianus*): Abundant throughout central New Mexico at lower elevations. One of the most reliable places to spot one is at the RGNC, where it is a resident breeder. It often will be seen in the Sandia Foothills, Petroglyph NM, Los Lunas River Park, Whitfield WCA, Bernardo WMA, and Bosque del Apache NWR.

Barn Owl (*Tyto alba*): Occasional in central New Mexico, where it nests in abandoned buildings or cliff cavities along I-25.

Flammulated Owl (*Otus flammeolus*): An uncommon summer resident in the Sandia Mountains, from Cienega Canyon on up the Sandia Crest Highway. One of the most reliable locations for this species at dusk is Capulin Spring Picnic Area.

Western Screech-Owl (*Megascops kennicottii*): An uncommon year-round resident and breeder in the Rio Grande bosque, mixed conifer forest, and piñon-juniper woodlands. Although nocturnal, it often perches in its cavity opening on warm, sunny days in early spring at the RGNC (check at the Visitor Center for the current year's location). Other locations include Elena Gallegos Open Space and Sulphur Canyon and Doc Long Picnic Areas.

Greater Roadrunner (Photo by Bonnie L. Long)

Great Horned Owl (*Bubo virginianus*): A common year-round resident and breeder throughout central New Mexico. Look for it roosting on the bare branches of a cottonwood tree along the middle Rio Grande. It also lives and nests among the boulders at the Petroglyph NM. One regularly nests at Quarai.

Northern Pygmy-Owl (*Glaucidium gnoma*): An occasional year-round resident, although not every year, along the Sandia Crest Highway in the Sandia Mountains.

Burrowing Owl (*Athene cunicularia*): An uncommon summer resident and breeder that is declining in central New Mexico due to habitat loss. It arrives in early March and generally has left by the end of September. It traditionally has nested behind the fast-food restaurant by the Belen Marsh. Other locations, not mentioned as specific sites in this book, include the Calabacitas Wash west of Golf Course Road NW, along Shooting Range Access Road NW west of the Petroglyph NM, and at the entrance to Sandia Casino. It is best to check eBird or the Rare Bird Alert (see chapter 2).

Northern Saw-whet Owl (*Aegolius acadicus*): An uncommon high-elevation resident that is often heard calling along the Sandia Crest Highway, particularly at Tree Springs Trailhead.

Lesser Nighthawk (*Chordeiles acutipennis*): Primarily a summer resident of southern New Mexico. Its range extends north to the Bosque del Apache NWR, where it is uncommon over the wetlands along with the Common Nighthawk between mid-April and mid-September, but primarily in the spring.

Common Nighthawk (*Chordeiles minor*): An uncommon migrant, as well as summer resident and breeder, in areas along the middle Rio Grande from May through September; often prevalent at dusk at Bosque del Apache NWR.

Common Poorwill (*Phalaenoptilus nuttallii*): An uncommon summer resident and breeder in foothill canyons and mountains, more easily heard than seen from May through September.

White-throated Swift (*Aeronautes saxatalis*): An uncommon summer resident that soars alongside cliffs and foothill canyons. Look for it in summer just below the crest of the Sandia Mountains from the Kiwanis Cabin overlook.

Black-chinned Hummingbird (*Archilochus alexandri*): A common summer resident and breeder in the lowlands, arriving in April and present

Great Horned Owl at Quarai

through September. The most prevalent hummingbird species at the RGNC and Bosque del Apache NWR feeders.

Calliope Hummingbird (*Stellula calliope*): An uncommon migrant, mid-July through mid-September, through both the mountains and the valley. The easiest place to observe one is at the Sandia Crest House feeders.

Broad-tailed Hummingbird (*Selasphorus platycercus*): A common summer resident and breeder at elevations above 6,000 feet; sometimes seen in the foothills and lowlands during migration. The most prevalent hummingbird species at the Sandia Crest House feeders.

Rufous Hummingbird (*Selasphorus rufus*): A common fall migrant, it begins arriving throughout central New Mexico on its southward migration during July and continues to migrate through the area until the end of September

Belted Kingfisher (*Megaceryle alcyon*): An uncommon year-round resident and breeder, particularly along the Rio Grande and nearby drainage ditches. It potentially can be seen at any of the sites along the river, from Corrales Bosque to the Bosque del Apache NWR.

Lewis's Woodpecker (*Melanerpes lewis*): Formerly a year-round resident in the town of Corrales and nearby bosque and in Los Lunas and Belen in dead and dying cottonwoods along the river; however, after these trees were cleared, its nesting sites disappeared. An uncommon fall migrant that is banded regularly at Capilla Peak.

Williamson's Sapsucker (*Sphyrapicus thyroideus*): Uncommon in mixed conifer forests of the Sandia, Manzanita, and Manzano Mountains year-round. Search for it at Sulphur Canyon or Doc Long Picnic Area and Otero and Fourth of July Canyons.

Red-naped Sapsucker (*Sphyrapicus nuchalis*): An uncommon summer resident and breeder in mixed conifer and ponderosa forests. During fall and winter, it moves to lower elevations, where it prefers elm trees. Look for it in the summer at Cienega Canyon, Sulphur Canyon and Doc Long Picnic

Rufous Hummingbird (Photo by Bonnie L. Long)

Areas, along the Sandia Crest Highway, and Capulin Spring; and in fall and winter at the Sandia District Ranger Station and Otero and Fourth of July Canyons.

Ladder-backed Woodpecker (*Picoides scalaris*): An uncommon year-round resident and breeder in desert scrub habitat of central New Mexico. Be alert for it in the Sandia Foothills and at Ojito de San Antonio Open Space, Quarai, and the Bosque del Apache NWR.

Downy Woodpecker (*Picoides pubescens*): A common year-round resident and breeder. Although more prevalent in deciduous habitats along the middle Rio Grande, it is an occasional visitor at higher elevations. Scan the trees at any of the sites along the river or at Ojito de San Antonio Open Space.

Hairy Woodpecker (*Picoides villosus*): A year-round resident and breeder that is more common at higher elevations. It occasionally winters at sites along the middle Rio Grande but is the most common woodpecker in the Sandia, Manzanita, and Manzano Mountains.

American Three-toed Woodpecker (*Picoides dorsalis*): An uncommon year-round resident and breeder in the Sandia Mountains at elevations above 10,000 feet, preferring dying Engelmann spruce. Search for it at Sandia Crest, at the Ellis Trailhead, and along the 10K Trail.

Northern Flicker (*Colaptes auratus*): The subspecies found in this area is "Red-shafted" (*C. a. cafer*). A common year-round resident and breeder found primarily at higher elevations during the summer months. It migrates to the valleys around mid-October and remains until mid-April. Depending upon the time of year, it is possible to spot this species at any of the sites.

Olive-sided Flycatcher (*Contopus cooperi*): An uncommon migrant through central New Mexico. Look for it in the spring (May) or fall (August and September) at sites along the middle Rio Grande, Cienega Canyon, or Quarai.

Western Wood-Pewee (*Contopus sordidulus*): A common summer resident and breeder at sites along the middle Rio Grande and in the Sandia, Manzanita, and Manzano Mountains.

Willow Flycatcher (*Empidonax traillii*): The federally designated endangered subspecies, "Southwestern" (*E. t. extimus*), migrates through central New Mexico and has been known to breed in the dense willows that grow under the cottonwoods along the middle Rio Grande as far north as Bernardo and has been observed at the Whitfield WCA.

Hammond's Flycatcher (*Empidonax hammondii*): An occasional migrant along the river and through the mountains of central New Mexico during the spring and fall. It is often confused with Dusky Flycatcher; the primary identifier is its vocalization.

Gray Flycatcher (*Empidonax wrightii*): An uncommon migrant through central New Mexico and common summer resident and breeder in Otero Canyon that arrives in April and remains through September.

Dusky Flycatcher (*Empidonax oberholseri*): An uncommon migrant through the valley, as well as summer resident and breeder at high-elevation forests. Look for it during the summer near the south 10K Trail (along the Sandia Crest Highway) or in the Capulin Snow Play Area (Capulin Spring).

Cordilleran Flycatcher (*Empidonax occidentalis*): A common summer resident and breeder in high-elevation, coniferous forests that arrives in May and remains through September. Search for it at any of the sites in the Sandia Mountains and in Tajique and Fourth of July Canyons.

Black Phoebe (*Sayornis nigricans*): A common year-round resident and breeder throughout the riparian lowlands from the Corrales Bosque to the Bosque del Apache NWR.

Say's Phoebe (*Sayornis saya*): Migrant through central New Mexico, as well as a common year-round resident and breeder at sites in the Sandia Foothills, at Petroglyph NM, and along the middle Rio Grande.

Vermilion Flycatcher (*Pyrocephalus rubinus*): Primarily found in riparian areas in southern New Mexico; however, it occasionally ventures north as far as the Bosque del Apache NWR, where it has been spotted at all times of the year.

Ash-throated Flycatcher (*Myiarchus cinerascens*): A common summer resident and breeder, arriving in late April and leaving in August. It can be found at sites along the middle Rio Grande and in the Sandia Foothills, Ojito de San Antonio Open Space, and Tajique and Fourth of July Canyons.

Cassin's Kingbird (*Tyrannus vociferans*): An uncommon summer resident and breeder, arriving in April and leaving by the end of September, found primarily in desert scrub and piñon-juniper habitats at higher elevations than the Western Kingbird. Seek this species at any of the Sandia Foothills sites, at the Sandia District Ranger Station, in Otero Canyon, or at Quarai.

Western Kingbird (*Tyrannus verticalis*): A common summer resident and breeder, arriving in mid-April and leaving in September. It is more prevalent in riparian lowlands, as well as at Petroglyph NM.

Loggerhead Shrike (*Lanius ludovicianus*): An uncommon year-round resident and breeder in desert scrub, grass, and farmlands. Look for it at Rinconada Canyon and along NM 1 south of the village of San Antonio just north of Bosque del Apache NWR.

Gray Vireo (*Vireo vicinior*): An uncommon summer resident and breeder, arriving from mid- to late April and generally departing by mid-August. The most reliable nesting locations are in a combined piñon-juniper and desert scrub habitat on Kirtland Air Force Base in Albuquerque, not generally open to the public. Unfortunately, other similar habitats in central New Mexico are sporadic and/or difficult to reach. The best time to spot one occurs when the male is singing on territory. Once it starts feeding the fledglings, it stops singing.

Plumbeous Vireo (*Vireo plumbeus*): A migrant along the middle Rio Grande and a common summer resident and breeder in mountain canyons with deciduous understory. It begins arriving in late April and leaves by the end of September. Search for it at lower elevations in the Sandia Mountains (Ojito de San Antonio Open Space, Sulphur Canyon and Doc Long Picnic Areas, and Cienega Canyon), and the Manzanita and Manzano Mountains (Otero Canyon, Manzano Pond, Tajique and Fourth of July Canyons, and Quarai).

Cassin's Vireo (*Vireo cassinii*): An occasional spring (mid-April through mid-May) and fall (primarily September) migrant along the river and in riparian pockets in the Sandia and Manzano Mountains, such as Quarai.

Warbling Vireo (*Vireo gilvus*): A migrant along the middle Rio Grande and a common summer resident and breeder in high-elevation forests in the Sandia, Manzanita, and Manzano Mountains. It arrives in early May and leaves by the end of September. Look for it at any of the sites in the Sandia, Manzanita, and Manzano Mountains. It overlaps with Plumbeous Vireo at lower elevations.

Pinyon Jay (*Gymnorhinus cyanocephalus*): Roving widely in flocks, it is an uncommon year-round resident and breeder in piñon-juniper habitat. It is a fairly regular winter visitor to the Copper Trailhead Open Space and is often seen along the Manzanita and Manzano Mountains.

Steller's Jay (*Cyanocitta stelleri*): A common year-round resident and breeder in the Sandia, Manzanita, and Manzano Mountains.

Western Scrub-Jay (*Aphelocoma californica*): The subspecies found in this area is "Woodhouse's" (*A. c. woodhouseii*). A common resident and breeder, primarily in desert scrub and piñon-juniper habitats. Look for it at any of the Sandia Foothills sites or along the Manzanita and Manzano Mountains.

Clark's Nutcracker (*Nucifraga columbiana*): An uncommon year-round resident and breeder at elevations above 8,000 feet, where its presence is variable. The most reliable location for spotting one is on the trail heading north of the Visitor Center at Sandia Crest.

American Crow (*Corvus brachyrhynchos*): An abundant year-round resident and breeder that feeds in large flocks in agricultural fields up and down the middle Rio Grande valley. In the winter, it communally roosts in the valley and often flies to the mountains during the day.

Chihuahuan Raven (*Corvus cryptoleucus*): An uncommon species of desert scrub habitat from the Bosque del Apache NWR north to the Petroglyph NM; identified primarily by its call. Look for it at the sites south of Albuquerque.

Common Raven (*Corvus corax*): A common year-round resident and breeder; however, it is much more prevalent during the winter.

Horned Lark (*Eremophila alpestris*): An uncommon winter resident in fields and agricultural areas and occasional summer resident. Scrutinize the plowed fields along the middle Rio Grande south to the Bosque del Apache NWR and along the Manzanita and Manzano Mountains.

Tree Swallow (*Tachycineta bicolor*): An occasional migrant in the spring starting in early March and in the fall from mid-July through October at sites along the middle Rio Grande.

Violet-green Swallow (*Tachycineta thalassina*): A migrant through the middle Rio Grande valley and a locally common summer resident and breeder at high elevations. Watch for it in the summer at sites along the Sandia Crest Highway up to the crest and at sites along the Manzanita and Manzano Mountains, Tajique and Fourth of July Canyons, and Quarai.

Northern Rough-winged Swallow (*Stelgidopteryx serripennis*): A common migrant, primarily along the middle Rio Grande. It is an uncommon summer resident and can be seen at selected areas, including the RGNC.

Bank Swallow (*Riparia riparia*): Primarily an uncommon migrant. Historically there has been a breeding colony in the Albuquerque area, and a few often swoop over the parking-lot pond at the RGNC during June and early July.

Cliff Swallow (*Petrochelidon pyrrhonota*): A migrant through central New Mexico and a common summer resident, nesting under bridges along the middle Rio Grande. It begins arriving in March, and most are gone by the end of August. Check the Alameda Open Space, Corrales Bosque, and all sites south of Albuquerque.

Barn Swallow (*Hirundo rustica*): An abundant migrant, summer resident, and breeder between mid-March and early October; the most common swallow at the RGNC. In addition to gleaning insects over ponds and wetlands, it patrols fields, the foothills, and mountain meadows.

Black-capped Chickadee (*Poecile atricapillus*): A common year-round resident in the cottonwood bosque habitat along the middle Rio Grande. It is possible to spot this species at any site along the river.

Mountain Chickadee (*Poecile gambeli*): A common year-round resident and breeder in coniferous forests; however, uncommon at lower elevations during the winter.

Juniper Titmouse (*Baeolophus ridgwayi*): A common year-round resident of piñon-juniper and pine-oak habitats. Look for it at Elena Gallegos Picnic Area, Three Gun Spring, Ojito de San Antonio Open Space, Sulphur Canyon and Doc Long Picnic Areas, Cienega Canyon, Sandia Ranger District Station, Otero Canyon, and Quarai.

Verdin (*Auriparus flaviceps*): An uncommon year-round resident in desert scrub habitat at the Bosque del Apache NWR.

Bushtit (*Psaltriparus minimus*): A common year-round resident and breeder along the middle Rio Grande, in the Sandia Foothills, in lower elevations in the Sandia and Manzanita Mountains, and at Quarai.

Red-breasted Nuthatch (*Sitta canadensis*): A common year-round resident and breeder in the Sandia, Manzanita, and Manzano Mountains, although occasionally it wanders through the lowlands during the winter.

White-breasted Nuthatch (*Sitta carolinensis*): A common year-round resident and breeder along the middle Rio Grande and in the mountains.

Pygmy Nuthatch (*Sitta pygmaea*): An uncommon year-round resident and breeder in the Sandia, Manzanita, and Manzano Mountains. Search in the ponderosas at Sulphur Canyon and Doc Long Picnic Areas, in Cienega Canyon, along the Sandia Crest Highway, and in ponderosa habitat in the Manzanita and Manzano Mountains.

Brown Creeper (*Certhia americana*): An uncommon year-round resident and breeder in the Sandia, Manzanita, and Manzano Mountains, although it sometimes migrates to lower elevations during fall and winter.

Cactus Wren (*Campylorhynchus brunneicapillus*): An uncommon year-round resident and breeder in cholla cactus in the Sandia Foothills that has nested at Embudo Canyon and the Copper Trailhead Open Space; can also be found in desert scrub habitat near the Bosque del Apache NWR.

Rock Wren (*Salpinctes obsoletus*): An uncommon summer resident in the Sandia Foothills and Otero Canyon; year-round resident and breeder in the Petroglyph NM and the desert scrub habitat at the Bosque del Apache NWR.

Canyon Wren (*Catherpes mexicanus*): An uncommon year-round resident and breeder in the canyons of the Sandia Foothills, Otero Canyon, and the Petroglyph NM.

Bewick's Wren (*Thryomanes bewickii*): A common year-round resident and breeder in the understory at all sites along the middle Rio Grande and in piñon-juniper habitat in the Sandia Foothills, Sandia District Ranger Station, Otero Canyon, and Quarai.

House Wren (*Troglodytes aedon*): A migrant along the middle Rio Grande and other sites at lower elevations, such as Quarai, as well as common summer resident and breeder at higher elevations in the Sandia Mountains.

Marsh Wren (*Cistothorus palustris*): A migrant through central New Mexico and uncommon winter resident in marshes. Listen for its buzzy call at the Alameda Open Space, RGNC, Belen Marsh, Whitfield WCA, Bernardo WMA, and Bosque del Apache NWR.

Golden-crowned Kinglet (*Regulus satrapa*): An uncommon year-round resident and breeder at elevations above 10,000 feet. Check high in the tops of corkbark fir along the 10K Trail, Sandia Crest, Fourth of July Canyon, and Capilla Peak.

Ruby-crowned Kinglet (*Regulus calendula*): A common summer resident and breeder at high altitudes in the Sandia and Manzano Mountains that migrates to lower elevations in the fall and spends the winter at sites along the middle Rio Grande and Sandia Foothills in piñon-juniper habitat.

Blue-gray Gnatcatcher (*Polioptila caerulea*): An uncommon migrant at foothill sites, along the middle Rio Grande, and at the Petroglyph NM, late March through May and mid-August through mid-October. A few are summer residents and breeders in piñon-juniper habitat at Three Gun Spring and Ojito de San Antonio Open Space.

Eastern Bluebird (*Sialia sialis*): An uncommon winter resident at sites along the middle Rio Grande. Small pockets remain year-round and breed, including at the RGNC.

Western Bluebird (*Sialia mexicana*): A common summer resident and breeder in piñon-juniper through mixed conifer habitats of open mountain areas of the Sandia, Manzanita, and Manzano Mountains, descending into the foothills and along the middle Rio Grande in September, remaining until mid-March. In the summer, you can easily see one at the 10K Trailhead (see "Along the Sandia Crest Highway"), and year-round all along the Manzanita and Manzano Mountains. In the winter, it is abundant at Elena Gallegos Picnic Area.

Mountain Bluebird (*Sialia currucoides*): There is a small population year-round, chiefly along NM 337 and NM 55, including Quarai; often seen in grassy habitat and agricultural fields during the winter, including Bosque del Apache NWR, Bernardo WMA, and west of Petroglyph NM.

Townsend's Solitaire (*Myadestes townsendi*): An uncommon resident fall through spring at sites in the Sandia Foothills and Otero Canyon.

Hermit Thrush (*Catharus guttatus*): A common summer resident, breeder, and spring and fall migrant in coniferous forests in the Sandia Mountains from Cienega Canyon to the Sandia Crest and in the Manzano Mountains at Fourth of July Canyon and Capilla Peak; also an uncommon winter resident at sites along the middle Rio Grande.

American Robin (*Turdus migratorius*): Common to abundant year-round. Because it is a short-distance migrant, there may be brief gaps between wintering and summering populations in some areas. It is present at all sites, except in desert scrub.

Gray Catbird (*Dumetella carolinensis*): Although there have been some reports of nesting along the middle Rio Grande, it is an occasional spring and fall migrant.

Northern Mockingbird (*Mimus polyglottos*): A migrant as well as uncommon summer resident and breeder in areas with desert scrub habitat.

Sage Thrasher (*Oreoscoptes montanus*): A migrant and uncommon winter resident in habitats dominated by sagebrush or piñon-juniper that is encountered occasionally in the Sandia Foothills, west of the Petroglyph NM, and the Chupadera Trail area of Bosque del Apache NWR.

Curve-billed Thrasher (*Toxostoma curvirostre*): A common year-round resident and breeder in desert scrub habitat containing cholla cactus that can be found at most Sandia Foothills sites. At times it can be spotted at the Petroglyph NM sites; however, it is not known to nest there.

Crissal Thrasher (*Toxostoma crissale*): An uncommon year-round resident and breeder in desert scrub habitat; found at Embudito, Embudo, Copper Trailhead, and Three Gun Open Spaces but is harder to find than the Curve-billed Thrasher. It is the only nesting thrasher at the two sites at Petroglyph NM.

European Starling (*Sturnus vulgaris*): A common year-round resident and breeder in central New Mexico.

American Pipit (*Anthus rubescens*): An uncommon winter resident and migrant between October and April. Look for it in flocks on agricultural

Sage Thrasher

fields. The best places to check are Whitfield WCA, Bernardo WMA, and along NM 1 from San Antonio to the Bosque del Apache NWR.

Cedar Waxwing (*Bombycilla cedrorum*): An uncommon migrant, often visiting the Rio Grande bosque during winter; also often seen in the winter at Ojito de San Antonio Open Space.

Phainopepla (*Phainopepla nitens*): An uncommon year-round resident and breeder at the Bosque del Apache NWR and a summer resident at Quarai.

Orange-crowned Warbler (*Oreothlypis celata*): A common migrant from early April through mid-May and August through October. In addition, it nests in the Sandia and Manzano Mountains at elevations above 8,000 feet.

Virginia's Warbler (*Oreothlypis virginiae*): A migrant along the middle Rio Grande, and occasionally in the foothills, from mid-April to mid-May and in September; also a common summer resident and breeder at middle elevations in the Sandia, Manzanita, and Manzano Mountains in locations where conifer forests mix with deciduous shrubs or trees from Sulphur and Cienega Canyons up to Capulin Spring and at Tajique and Fourth of July Canyons.

Lucy's Warbler (*Oreothlypis luciae*): An uncommon desert riparian species. Bosque del Apache NWR is normally the northern end of its range; however, occasionally it is seen along the middle Rio Grande up to Bernardo WMA. It arrives in early April and stays through the end of July.

Yellow Warbler (*Dendroica petechia*): An uncommon migrant through riparian areas, primarily along the middle Rio Grande in April and May and mid-August through mid-September. It nests at the Bosque del Apache NWR.

Yellow-rumped Warbler (*Dendroica coronata*): The "Audubon's" race (*D. c. auduboni*) is a common summer resident and breeder in the Sandia Mountains from Cienega and Sulphur Canyons up to the crest, and in the Manzano Mountains at Tajique and Fourth of July Canyons. Both races, "Myrtle" (*D. c. coronata*) and "Audubon's," are common winter residents and migrants, primarily along the middle Rio Grande.

Black-throated Gray Warbler (*Dendroica nigrescens*): An uncommon summer resident and breeder in piñon-juniper habitat that arrives in mid-April and starts leaving in late August. It breeds in Ojito de San Antonio Open Space and Otero Canyon.

Townsend's Warbler (*Dendroica townsendi*): An uncommon fall migrant through the Sandia, Manzanita, and Manzano Mountains: at Capulin Spring and Sulphur, Cienega, Otero, and Fourth of July Canyons from mid-August through the end of September.

Grace's Warbler (*Dendroica graciae*): A common summer resident and breeder in ponderosa pine habitat, arriving mid-April and leaving by mid-September. Search in the Sandia Mountains at sites between Sulphur and Cienega Canyons up to Capulin Spring and at Fourth of July Canyon in the Manzano Mountains.

Northern Waterthrush (*Parkesia noveboracensis*): An occasional spring and fall migrant in the understory along the middle Rio Grande and at Quarai.

MacGillivray's Warbler (*Oporornis tolmiei*): An uncommon summer resident and breeder in the Sandia Mountains from Sulphur and Cienega Canyons up to Sandia Crest and in the Manzano Mountains at Tajique and Fourth of July Canyons. It migrates through the lowlands in May and late August to early October, frequenting low shrubs near water.

Common Yellowthroat (*Geothlypis trichas*): A fairly common summer resident and breeder in marshy habitats, mostly at sites along the middle Rio Grande. It also migrates through central New Mexico in these same habitats.

Wilson's Warbler (*Wilsonia pusilla*): A common migrant along the middle Rio Grande and lower mountains from mid-April through May and mid-August through early October.

Yellow-breasted Chat (*Icteria virens*): A migrant through central New Mexico and a common summer resident and breeder at sites along the middle Rio Grande and at Quarai. It arrives at the end of April and stays through September.

Green-tailed Towhee (*Pipilo chlorurus*): An uncommon summer resident and breeder primarily in subalpine meadows in the Sandia Mountains, from the Sandia Ski Area up to Sandia Crest. It migrates through the valley during April and May and in September.

Spotted Towhee (*Pipilo maculatus*): An abundant year-round resident and breeder in habitats with dense shrubs and abundant leaf litter.

Canyon Towhee (*Melozone fusca*): A common year-round resident and breeder at sites in the Sandia Foothills, Ojito de San Antonio Open Space, Sandia District Ranger Station, Otero Canyon, Quarai, and sites at Petroglyph NM.

Rufous-crowned Sparrow (*Aimophila ruficeps*): An uncommon year-round resident and breeder at sites in the Sandia Foothills, Petroglyph NM, and desert scrub habitat at the Bosque del Apache NWR. Search in the rocky areas at the periphery of canyons.

Chipping Sparrow (*Spizella passerina*): An uncommon summer resident and breeder at mid- and upper-level forested areas in the Sandia, Manzanita, and Manzano Mountains. Soon after nesting, it disperses and is found widely in central New Mexico. During April and May and August through early October, it migrates through the valleys and foothill areas of central New Mexico.

Clay-colored Sparrow (*Spizella pallida*): An occasional migrant seen regularly during September in open brushy areas or grasslands, although not at any particular site.

Brewer's Sparrow (*Spizella breweri*): An uncommon migrant mid-April through mid-May and in September, most often in bushy desert scrub habitats, including the Sandia Foothills and sites at Petroglyph NM.

Black-chinned Sparrow (*Spizella atrogularis*): An uncommon summer resident and breeder in the Sandia Foothills, arriving in early April and departing by mid-August. It prefers dense desert scrub near the rocky edges of canyons.

Vesper Sparrow (*Pooecetes gramineus*): An occasional migrant from mid-March through mid-May and late August through mid-October in grassland and sagebrush habitats. Look along the Manzanita and Manzano Mountains and Petroglyph NM.

Lark Sparrow (*Chondestes grammacus*): An uncommon migrant from mid-April through June and from August through September. A good place to spot this species is along the Manzanita and Manzano Mountains, Whitfield WCA, and Bernardo WMA.

Black-throated Sparrow (*Amphispiza bilineata*): A common breeder in desert scrub habitat of the Sandia Foothills, at the Petroglyph NM sites, and along the Chupadera Trail at the Bosque del Apache NWR. It arrives in early March and remains until late fall.

Sage Sparrow (*Amphispiza belli*): A few Sage Sparrows spend the winter in the sagebrush of desert scrub habitat at Petroglyph NM and in the area of the Chupadera Trail at the Bosque del Apache NWR. The species arrives in mid-October and remains through March.

Savannah Sparrow (*Passerculus sandwichensis*): An occasional migrant and winter visitor seen in grassland habitat, including the fields adjacent to the Candelaria Wetlands at RGNC, Whitfield WCA, and Bosque del Apache NWR.

Song Sparrow (*Melospiza melodia*): A migrant through central New Mexico and a common winter resident at sites along the middle Rio Grande. It begins arriving in mid-September and stays through April or May, with the greatest abundance occurring in December.

Lincoln's Sparrow (*Melospiza lincolnii*): An occasional migrant and winter visitor along the middle Rio Grande.

White-throated Sparrow (*Zonotrichia albicollis*): An occasional visitor during the winter in flocks of White-crowned Sparrows at sites along the middle Rio Grande, but not predictably at any location. Scan each flock of White-crowned Sparrows carefully.

White-crowned Sparrow (*Zonotrichia leucophrys*): A widespread migrant and abundant winter resident in the Sandia Foothills, near Quarai, and all along the middle Rio Grande.

Chestnut-collared Longspur (*Calcarius ornatus*): An occasional winter visitor to grassland habitat between October and March, often found in mixed flocks with Horned Larks and American Pipits.

Dark-eyed Junco (*Junco hyemalis*): The "Gray-headed" race (*J. h. caniceps*) is a common summer resident and breeder primarily above 6,500 feet in the Sandia, Manzanita, and Manzano Mountains. In mid-September, migrants arrive in the lowlands, primarily "Oregon" (*J. h. oreganus*), along with "Gray-headed," "Pink-sided" (*J. h. mearnsi*), and "Slate-colored" (*J. h. hyemalis*), and can be found occasionally at sites along the middle Rio Grande.

Hepatic Tanager (*Piranga flava*): An occasional summer resident in pine and pine-oak woodlands, arriving in early May and leaving by the end of August; not seen consistently at any one location.

Summer Tanager (*Piranga rubra*): A common summer resident and breeder in the cottonwood bosque at sites all along the middle Rio Grande. It arrives in late April and stays through the end of September.

Western Tanager (*Piranga ludoviciana*): An uncommon summer resident and breeder at moderate and high elevations. In the Sandia Mountains it can be found from Ojito de San Antonio Open Space up to the Sandia Crest. In the Manzano Mountains it is found along the Tunnel Spring Trail at Otero and at Fourth of July Canyons and Quarai. It migrates through sites along the middle Rio Grande in May and mid-August through mid-September.

Pyrrhuloxia (*Cardinalis sinuatus*): Uncommon from late October through April in desert scrub habitat at the Bosque del Apache NWR, the traditional northern edge of its range. It sometimes wanders during the winter and occasionally might be spotted at locations farther north.

Black-headed Grosbeak (*Pheucticus melanocephalus*): A common summer resident and breeder in riparian habitat all along the middle Rio Grande, as well as in the Sandia, Manzanita, and Manzano Mountains up through the mixed conifer habitat. It arrives in early May and stays through mid-September.

Blue Grosbeak (*Passerina caerulea*): A common summer resident and breeder in riparian areas all along the middle Rio Grande and foothill riparian areas, such as Cedro Nature Trail and Quarai. It arrives in early May and leaves by early October.

Lazuli Bunting (*Passerina amoena*): An uncommon and inconsistent migrant, summer resident, and breeder in riparian areas with brushy understory along the middle Rio Grande and in foothill riparian areas such as Ojito de San Antonio Open Space and Quarai. It arrives in late April and remains through September.

Red-winged Blackbird (*Agelaius phoeniceus*): An abundant year-round resident and breeder in marshes and wet fields. Find this species at the RGNC, Corrales Bosque, Manzano Pond, Quarai, Mountainair sewage ponds, Belen Marsh, Whitfield WCA, Bernardo WMA, and Bosque del Apache NWR.

Eastern Meadowlark (*Sturnella magna*): Seen occasionally in grassland habitat, including west of the Petroglyph NM and the Bosque del Apache NWR.

Western Meadowlark (*Sturnella neglecta*): Common year-round resident in grasslands and agricultural fields, at Whitfield WCA, and along the tour route edges at Bosque del Apache NWR.

Yellow-headed Blackbird (*Xanthocephalus xanthocephalus*): An uncommon migrant through central New Mexico in lesser numbers during March and April, and more abundantly during late August through September, often mixed with Red-winged Blackbirds. An occasional summer breeder, it is a common winter resident at the Bosque del Apache NWR, often in mixed flocks.

Brewer's Blackbird (*Euphagus cyanocephalus*): A common migrant and winter resident in the valley and along the middle Rio Grande.

Great-tailed Grackle (*Quiscalus mexicanus*): A widespread year-round resident and breeder in lowland areas along the middle Rio Grande and locally on golf courses. During the breeding season, it often shares breeding habitat with Red-winged Blackbirds.

Brown-headed Cowbird (*Molothrus ater*): A common summer resident and breeder, where its nest parasitism has been documented on a number of Breeding Bird Surveys, including Doc Long Picnic Area and Otero, Tajique, and Fourth of July Canyons. It arrives in early April and is gone by the end of September.

Bullock's Oriole (*Icterus bullockii*): A common migrant, summer resident, and breeder in riparian woodlands along the middle Rio Grande and in the foothills. It begins to arrive in late April and is present through early September.

Scott's Oriole (*Icterus parisorum*): An uncommon summer resident and breeder in canyons of the Sandia Foothills, including Embudito, Embudo, Copper Trailhead, and Three Gun. It arrives in mid-April and has left by the end of August.

Gray-crowned Rosy-Finch (*Leucosticte tephrocotis*): A common winter visitor seen at the Crest House feeders that arrives in early November and leaves by mid- to late March. Flocks often contain a few Hepburn's subspecies (*L. t. littoralis*).

Black Rosy-Finch (*Leucosticte atrata*): A common rosy-finch in the mixed flocks that visit the feeders at the Crest House.

Brown-capped Rosy-Finch (*Leucosticte australis*): A common winter visitor at Sandia Crest with the other two species.

Pine Grosbeak (*Pinicola enucleator*): An occasional and irregular winter visitor at elevations above 10,000 feet in the Sandia Mountains.

Cassin's Finch (*Carpodacus cassinii*): Seen primarily in the Sandia Mountains during fall and winter, where it is uncommon. In some years, it is more plentiful than in others. During irruptive years, it is often spotted in the lowlands.

House Finch (*Carpodacus mexicanus*): An abundant year-round resident and breeder at sites along the Rio Grande and in the foothills.

Red Crossbill (*Loxia curvirostra*): An uncommon year-round resident and breeder at high elevations in the Sandia, Manzanita, and Manzano Mountains that roves in flocks, making it difficult to specify any particular location to find it.

Pine Siskin (*Spinus pinus*): A common year-round resident and breeder in the Sandia, Manzanita, and Manzano Mountains and foothills. It may migrate to lower elevations during fall and winter.

Lesser Goldfinch (*Spinus psaltria*): A common migrant, summer resident, and breeder at all but the highest elevations. In some areas, it is a year-round resident.

American Goldfinch (*Spinus tristis*): A common winter resident at sites all along the middle Rio Grande.

Evening Grosbeak (*Coccothraustes vespertinus*): An occasional year-round resident in the Sandia, Manzanita, and Manzano Mountains.

House Sparrow (*Passer domesticus*): An abundant introduced resident in populated areas.

Selected Resources

American Birding Association. 2010. *Code of birding ethics*. Colorado Springs: American Birding Association. Available at www.aba.org.

Cartron, J., D. Lightfoot, J. Mygatt, S. Brantley, and T. Lowrey. 2008. *A field guide to the plants and animals of the middle Rio Grande bosque*. Albuquerque: University of New Mexico Press.

Coltrain, M. 2005. *Sandia Mountain hiking guide*. Albuquerque: University of New Mexico Press.

eBird. 2009. eBird: An online database of bird distribution and abundance [web application]. Version 2. Ithaca, N.Y.: eBird. Available at www.ebird.org.

Ehrlich, P., D. Dobkin, and D. Wheye. 1988. The birder's handbook: *A field guide to the natural history of North American birds*. New York: Simon and Schuster.

Julyan, R., and M. Stuever, eds. 2005. *Field guide to the Sandia Mountains*. Albuquerque: University of New Mexico Press.

Kelly, V. C. 1982. *Albuquerque, its mountains, valley, water and volcanoes*. Socorro: New Mexico Bureau of Mines and Mineral Resources.

Morris, L., M. Stuever, L. Ellis, and R. Tydings, eds. 2006. *Bosque education guide*. 2d ed. Albuquerque: Friends of the Rio Grande Nature Center.

Parmeter, J., B. Neville, and D. Emkalns. 2002. *New Mexico bird finding guide*. 3d ed. Albuquerque: New Mexico Ornithological Society.

Patuxent Wildlife Research Center. 2009. *Breeding bird atlas explorer*. Patuxent, Md.: Patuxent Wildlife Research Center. Available at www.pwrc.usgs.gov/bba/index.cfm?fa=bba.About.

Rosner, J., and H. Rosner. 1996. *Albuquerque's environmental story: Toward a sustainable community*. Albuquerque: Cottonwood Printing. Available at www.cabq.gov/aes/acredit.html.

Rustay, C., and S. Norris, comps. 2007. *New Mexico bird conservation plan.* Version 2.1. Albuquerque: New Mexico Partners in Flight. Available at www.nmpartnersinflight.org/species.html.

Sibley, D. A. 2003. *The Sibley field guide to birds of western North America.* New York: Alfred A. Knopf.

Index

Photos and maps are indicated with *italic* type.

agricultural
   sites with, 19, 21, 23, 26, 131
   species found in, 162, 163, 164,
      177, 180, 181, 186
Chihuahuan/upland desert scrub
   sites with, 36, 50, 46, *50,* 52, 62,
      150, 155
   species found in, 174, 175, 176,
      177, 178, 179, 180, 181, 184,
      186
mixed conifer forest
   sites with, 68, 75, 86, 97
   species found in, 173, 175, 180,
      186
middle-elevation riparian
   sites with, 19, 28, 35
montane riparian
   sites with, 68, 69, 78
piñon-juniper woodland/forest
   sites with, 39, 40, 68, 69, 97,
      103, 105, 117, 118, 121
   species found in, 170, 175, 176,
      177, 178, 179, 180, 182
spruce-fir forest
   sites with, 68, 74, 91, 115
subalpine meadow
   sites with, 75, 91
   species found in, 183
transition/ponderosa pine forest
   sites with. 68, 75, 78, 83, 111
   species found in, 173, 178, 183
wetlands/lakes
   sites with, 19, 23, 26 28, 99,
      131, 135, 136, 138, 140, 147,
      148, 149, 150, 153, 154
   species found in, 162, 163, 164,
      165, 166, 167, 168, 169, 171,
      179, 183, 186
Harrier, Northern, 21, 153, 165

Hawk
   Broad-winged, 116, 166
   Cooper's, 19, 21, 26, 31, 32, 36,
      42, 49, 55, 61, 66, 81, 84, 114,
      125, 128, 133, 141, 166
   Ferruginous, 116, 155, 166
   Red-tailed, 21, 26, 49, 55, 61, 101,
      104, 115, 125, 133, 141, 146,
      153, 166
   Rough-legged, 116, 166
   Sharp-shinned, 21, 66, 114, 166
   Swainson's, 115, 120, 125, 141,
      154, 166
HawkWatch, Manzano. *See* Capilla
   Peak and Manzano HawkWatch
HawkWatch, Sandia. *See* Three Gun
   Spring (Tres Pistolas) and
   HawkWatch Trails
HawkWatch International, 62–63, 114
Heron
   Black-crowned Night- (*see* Night-
      Heron, Black-crowned)
   Great Blue, 21, 26, 36, 141, 151, 164
   Green, 22, 26, 141, 154, 165
Hummingbird
   Black-chinned, 20, 26, 32, 36, 42,
      44, 50, 55, 61, 66, 71, 85, 120,
      125, 128, 133, 137, 141, 172
   Broad-tailed, 42, 50, 66, 71, 79,
      80, 85, 95, 104, 112, 120, 141, 172
   Calliope, 85, 92, 172
   Rufous, 32, 50, 55, 66, 85, 95, 141,
      172, *173*

Ibis
   Glossy, 136, 140, 165
   White-faced, 26, 32, 136, 140,
      154, 165
Important Bird Area, 105, 111, 114